Holy MOMENTS

WHEN LIFE AND FAITH INTERSECT

MARTHA DALTON WARD

WESTBOW
PRESS®
A DIVISION OF THOMAS NELSON
& ZONDERVAN

Scripture quotations are from the New Revised Standard Version Bible, copyright © 1989 the Division of Christian Education of the National Council of the Churches of Christ in the United States of America. Used by permission. All rights reserved.

Scripture taken from the King James Version of the Bible.

WestBow Press books may be ordered through booksellers or by contacting:

WestBow Press
A Division of Thomas Nelson & Zondervan
1663 Liberty Drive
Bloomington, IN 47403
www.westbowpress.com
1 (866) 928-1240

Because of the dynamic nature of the Internet, any web addresses or links contained in this book may have changed since publication and may no longer be valid. The views expressed in this work are solely those of the author and do not necessarily reflect the views of the publisher, and the publisher hereby disclaims any responsibility for them.

Any people depicted in stock imagery provided by Getty Images are models, and such images are being used for illustrative purposes only. Certain stock imagery © Getty Images.

ISBN: 978-1-9736-3281-8 (sc)
ISBN: 978-1-9736-3282-5 (hc)
ISBN: 978-1-9736-3280-1 (e)

Library of Congress Control Number: 2018907911

Print information available on the last page.

WestBow Press rev. date: 07/06/2018

Contents

Preface and Acknowledgments

For thirty-four years, I led weekly worship in United Methodist churches in Iowa. Co-pastoring for thirty-one of those years with my husband, Bob, I preached about half the Sundays. I regarded preaching as one of the most important, most challenging, and most humbling tasks of my ministry. My practice was to study the Scripture and to pray for insights that would speak to the faith journeys of those in our congregations.

When sermon ideas came, I asked myself, *Is this insight something I know about from my own history?* In searching my memories of family stories and of personal experiences, I often found a connection with the sermon theme of the week. Not all those memories put me or my family members in a positive light, but I preached the stories anyway and found that my honest confessions, foolish adventures, real-life struggles, and even mundane moments often spoke to the worshippers in a helpful way, encouraging them to grow in their relationship with God.

While studying Christian writers and theologians, I've noted how often biography is theology. For example, much of the church father Augustine's theology flowed from early experiences of his own sin; the faith and the beliefs of Methodism's founder, John Wesley, were energized in 1738 following a terrible failure in the American colonies. In *The Alphabet of Grace*, theologian Frederick Buechner put it like this: "Most theology, like most fiction, is essentially autobiography. Aquinas, Calvin, Barth, Tillich, worked out their systems in their own ways and lived them in their lives. And if you press them far enough, even at the most cerebral and forbidding, you will find an experience of flesh and blood, a human face smiling or frowning or weeping or covering its eyes before something that happened once ... maybe no more than a child falling sick, a thunderstorm, or a dream, and yet it made ... a difference which no theology can ever convey or entirely conceal."[1]

Our life stories greatly influence how each of us understands God. In this book, I have used personal and family stories from my sermons, along with Scripture verses, as a way of reflecting on my life and on what God has taught me.

Most of my life stories have been shared by my co-partner in marriage and ministry, Bob Ward. I dedicate this book to him with deep gratitude. I am also grateful to our son, David, who often allowed us to use experiences from his life as sermon examples. And I offer thanks to members of our extended family, who lived many of these stories, and to our friends and mentors along life's journey.

My hope is that these "holy moments" from my life might lead those who read about them to reflect on what God wants to teach them through their life stories.

CHAPTER 1

Our Everywhere God

Don't Put God in a Box

> But Moses said to God, "If I come to the Israelites and say to them, 'The God of your ancestors has sent me to you,' and they ask me, 'What is his name?' what shall I say to them?" God said to Moses, "I AM WHO I AM." He said further, "Thus you shall say to the Israelites, 'I AM has sent me to you.'" (Ex. 3:13–14)[1]

God has many names. In that way God reminds me a little of my maternal grandmother. Now, mind you, I'm not saying my grandmother was like God, although she was a wonderful person. She reminds me of God because she had a lot of names. Her parents named her Myrtle Vesta Maxwell. But my grandmother was not content with just those names. Somehow, they did not describe everything she was or might become.

And so, at various stages of her life, my grandmother took on new names—ones that fit who she was at those times: Myrtle, Vesta, Elizabeth, Jane, Psyche (how I would like to have known her when she was going by that name!), Nelson, Maxine, Maxwell, and

1

Krehbiel (her last name when she married my grandfather, B. F. Krehbiel). She kept all those names as parts of her formal name. They described some of the diversity of who she was. But of course, to us grandkids, she was always just plain Mamo—a name of endearment, of relationship, much like Jesus called God Abba—papa, or daddy. That's who she was to me, but I knew that in many ways she was much more; her character was multifaceted.

God is like that, only much, much more. Most of us have a special name we use for God—one that speaks to us of our relationship to God. Maybe the title we use is loving Creator, or heavenly Father, or merciful Lord, or blessed Savior. Whatever the name may be, we must always understand that God is much more than just that one special name. And if we limit ourselves to only one or two titles for God, we may be limiting the ways we experience our multifaceted God.

In the Bible, there are dozens of names for God. Here's what is important to remember: God will be for us what is best for us. We don't always recognize God's presence because we want to decide what is best for us rather than to let God show us. We want God on our own terms and don't want to accept the God who says, "I am who I am; I will be who I will be." But if we open ourselves up to this greatness and diversity of God, we will experience a power and a richness in our lives that is beyond naming.

Mechthild of Magdeburg, a thirteenth-century German mystic, wrote a beautiful prayer in that spirit:

> O burning Mountain, O Chosen Sun,
> O perfect Moon, O fathomless Well,
> O unattainable Height, O Clearness beyond measure,
> O Wisdom without end, O Mercy without limit,
> O Strength beyond resistance, O Crown beyond all majesty,

The humblest thing you created sings your praise.
Amen.²

You Belong to God

> Remember these things, O Jacob, and Israel, for you
> are my servant; I formed you, you are my servant; O
> Israel, you will not be forgotten by me. I have swept
> away your transgressions like a cloud, and your sins
> like mist; return to me, for I have redeemed you.
> (Isa. 44:21–22)

"Remember who you are." That's a phrase parents sometimes say
as they send their teenagers out into the world. Think of the high
values and morals in your lineage, and live up to them.

As a young person, I didn't like it when my grandfather Orville
Dalton (Gramps to me), would tell us how we were related to the
notorious Dalton Gang, a band of bank robbers and thieves who
met their demise in an 1892 shootout on Main Street in Coffeeville,
Kansas. In fact, when I later received an official genealogy of our
Dalton family, I was somewhat relieved to find the gang was not in
my family tree. The proposed connection had simply been teasing
by my fun-loving grandfather. But even if we had been related, that
would not have established who we were. Isaiah proclaims instead
that we are to remember we are beloved children of God, who
redeems us no matter what our sins or those of our ancestors.

God's Rescue Is Real

> In you, O Lord, I take refuge; let me never be put to
> shame. In your righteousness deliver me and rescue
> me; incline your ear to me and save me. Be to me a

> rock of refuge, a strong fortress, to save me, for you
> are my rock and my fortress. (Ps. 71:1–3)

God cares about us not just when we are faithful followers but even in our moments of great foolishness and of human weakness. My husband, Bob, and I learned that lesson well during a summer vacation in the late 1970s. During the long seminary break from the mid-May ending of the spring quarter until the beginning of the July summer term, we took a cross-country driving trip.

We found ourselves in Maine in early June, driving alongside an incredibly beautiful river, the Kennebeck. Bob and I considered ourselves to be pretty good canoeists—white-water enthusiasts. Thus, every time the highway took us over the Kennebeck, we wanted more and more to hop in a canoe and to run the river.

We didn't have a canoe with us, so we stopped at a small-town sporting goods store to see whether we could rent one. The people at the store said sure, but they didn't have a river canoe with a V-shaped keel for maneuvering through rapids; all they had was one flat-bottomed fiberglass canoe, which was designed for lake use. "That's okay," we said. "We're good canoeists—we can handle it." Then we inquired about life jackets. "All we have are these flotation cushions," they answered. "That's okay," we said. "We'll use those." They asked us whether anyone was joining us, and we replied, "Nope. We're on our own."

And so we were off. That June day was cool, so we were warmly dressed in jeans and flannel shirts. The river was running high and fast after spring rains. And it was beautiful! We went through some little riffles (small waves), and the canoe started picking up speed. The flat-bottomed canoe was a little harder for us to maneuver than usual, but we were doing fine. Then we hit the rapids. They looked manageable at the outset, but soon the waves became so high that they swamped the canoe. In a matter of moments, we capsized into the chilly water.

Our heads popped up above the surface of the water just in time

4

to see our two flotation cushions rush by in the rapid current. I had been in the bow of the canoe and thus was able to grab the canoe and hang on as it shot by. But that wasn't true for Bob, who had been in the stern. Upstream, he thrashed around in the river, weighed down by heavy clothes, breathless from the cold water—in trouble.

If you've ever been in fast-moving white water, you know the force of the water is incredibly powerful. I don't know exactly how to describe what happened next except to give my own interpretation. It was as though a power beyond me reached down and worked with me to swing the bow of the canoe upstream against the full force of the river so Bob could grab hold. Then the two of us held on until we could maneuver the upturned canoe and ourselves to shore and safety.

We got out and huddled together, wet and cold, fully aware of our foolishness—and enormously grateful that we worshipped a God who looks down on foolish creatures such as us and at times seems to intervene when it's obvious we are in over our heads! We pulled the canoe out of the water and carried it through the woods to our car—colder, wetter, but wiser. Thank goodness God does not leave us stranded and drowning in our own foolishness but with compassion is willing to intervene and to steer us back to shore.

Count Your Blessings

> Bless the Lord, O my soul, and all that is within me, bless his holy name. Bless the Lord, O my soul, and do not forget all his benefits—who forgives all your iniquity, who heals all your diseases, who redeems your life from the Pit, who crowns you with steadfast love and mercy. (Ps. 103:1–4)

Many of our blessings are fleeting—but not all. Some last forever. Those blessings came into sharp focus at Thanksgiving in

1979 during our last year of seminary in Berkeley, California. Since traveling to be with family in the Midwest was expensive, typically during seminary we shared a Thanksgiving meal with some of our fellow students. Not that year. Everyone had other plans, and we were going to be alone. So we decided to try something totally different—we would fast on Thanksgiving Day. Fasting is one of the classical spiritual disciplines. John Wesley, Methodism's founder, called it a means of grace—a way we can grow closer to God. We decided to try it. Some friends who were traveling offered us their home in Oakland as a site for our fast. We accepted and looked forward to the day of spiritual renewal.

Thanksgiving Day dawned cool and rainy, which should have been our first clue that the day would be a challenge. We had anticipated walking around the neighborhood. Now that seemed less desirable. We arrived at our friends' empty house, built a fire in the fireplace, and began what I still remember as one of the longest days of my life. We found comfy chairs, pulled out our Bibles and devotional books, and settled in for a time of fasting and prayer, but as the morning turned into the afternoon, my thoughts seemed drawn to one dominant image: Thanksgiving dinner—turkey, dressing, pumpkin pie. I pictured our loved ones around a huge table, enjoying the company and the food, and I wanted to be there. Fasting on a day when everyone else was feasting was probably not the best idea, especially for those of us who didn't fast regularly.

It was very hard! We fasted not only from food but from family and friends, and I remember it as a lonely day. But it's a Thanksgiving I will never forget. As we sat in an unfamiliar house on a dreary day, I made a long list of my blessings, and I recall feeling a profound sense of God's presence. I was thankful in a different way than I was on Thanksgivings surrounded by family and friends. Sometimes when our outer blessings are stripped away, we can experience more clearly the blessings we have from God, and those are the blessings we can count on.

God Is Always with Us

> Yea, though I walk through the valley of the shadow
> of death, I will fear no evil: for thou art with me; thy
> rod and thy staff they comfort me. (Ps. 23:4 KJV)[3]

I was terrified at the time. However, looking back, I can see how being the victim of an act of senseless violence opened my life to a profound sense of God's presence.

The year was 1980. I was a fresh new minister, two months into my first pastoral appointment in Waterloo, Iowa, when a man came to the small church I served, Graves United Methodist Church, requesting financial assistance. My office was in the basement of that aging church building behind the fellowship hall, down the hall next to the men's restroom and the boiler room. The office was very small—not unlike a large broom closet—but it was an office. There I sat at my desk, alone in the church, preparing my sermon. I had left the outside church door unlocked, signifying that the pastor was in.

It is not unusual for people seeking financial help to stop by churches. So I was not alarmed when the man entered the church, came to my office, sat down in the chair beside my desk, and said he needed money for essentials. I told him that our small congregation had no fund for financial assistance but that several agencies in town might be able to help him. As I sent him on his way with some written referrals, he asked to use the restroom. I returned to my sermon writing, and when the man left the restroom, he approached me with a knife in his hand.

Looking back, I am disappointed by my response to this situation. I wish I had jumped into action immediately, but my fear paralyzed me. I thought, *This kind of thing happens only on TV, not in real life. This can't be happening to me!* It wasn't until the man's knife had made a six-inch cut across the front of my neck that I told myself, *This is not a dream. It's a matter of life and death.* The man held the knife with one hand and one of my wrists with the other.

With my free hand, I tried to open the basement stairwell door that led outside from my office, but it was fastened with a dead bolt that had been painted shut. The man positioned himself between me and the exit. I felt trapped.

Words cannot fully describe my experience in the next few moments, but it was probably the most powerful experience of my life. I had a strong sense that this man and I were not the only ones in the room. My dingy little office suddenly seemed like holy ground, filled with the power and the presence of God. I felt a great peace—as though God's arms encircled me and a voice said to me, "Whatever happens here, I am with you. You are not alone."

And at that moment, I began to think clearly. I grabbed the man's other arm and said, "Drop that knife." Amazingly, he did. Perhaps he felt that power in the room too. Then, with our arms still locked, I dragged this man (who was larger than I was) from my office and across the fellowship hall, where it became clear to him that we were about to go up the stairs and out the side door. He panicked and fled toward another exit as I ran out the door to get help. The grocer across the street was shocked to see a young woman with a bleeding neck race into his store, but soon I was in an ambulance on my way to the hospital. My attacker was arrested shortly thereafter and later tried and convicted of this crime.

What I hope you take away from this story is not that I had a terrifying experience that came out all right but that in my most fearful moment, God was with me in the most powerful way I have ever experienced and that no matter what might have happened, I would have been in God's hands. God is with us! We are never alone. "Even though I walk through the valley of the shadow of death, thou art with me."

With God at Our Side

With the Lord on my side I do not fear. (Ps. 118:6)

In 1980 while in my first year of ministry and still recovering from a physical attack in my church office, a young friend gave me a plaque that is important to me even today. It says simply, "Lord, you and I can handle anything together." I needed that message then, for it came at a time when my fear and my faith were in hand-to-hand combat.

I needed the reminder of that plaque throughout my ministry, for I often had days when I felt I'd rather do it my way than put my faith in the unknown of God's love. Perhaps that's a message our world needs to hear—that if we would simply have faith in God's power and presence with us, maybe we could solve some of our problems. "Lord, you and I can handle anything together."

God Works for Good in All Circumstances

> We know that all things work together for good for those who love God, who are called according to his purpose. (Rom. 8:28)

From 1992 to 2000, Bob and I served as co-pastors at First United Methodist Church in Knoxville, Iowa, a town of around eight thousand people. One experience during our ministry there reminded me of how God multiplies our efforts when we seek to help those in need. Here's the story.

Knoxville had an active ecumenical food pantry that many of the area churches supported. The pantry had no paid staff but was blessed with a wonderful retired Baptist pastor, who volunteered there full time. I was a member of the pantry's board of directors when we were given an interesting fundraising opportunity.

Knoxville is the Marion County seat but is not the largest town in the county. That's Pella, a thriving community with several large employers. One of them was holding a summer employee appreciation day on its expansive grounds. It was to be a Saturday carnival with rides and bounce houses for the kids and food and drink for the adults. All Marion County nonprofits were invited to serve as food vendors. Our food pantry had never done that before, but we decided to give it a try. We would serve pie and ice cream, inviting all the Knoxville churches to donate home-baked pies. Church people love to bake pies, and we easily recruited more than two hundred pies, all carefully stored in our Methodist church kitchen.

A small committee (the retired Baptist pastor, a wonderful Catholic laywoman, and I) formulated a plan. We bought large containers of ice cream and stored them in our food pantry freezers. Our retired pastor agreed to load the large freezers in his truck and to haul them to Pella the Friday before the event. The freezers could be plugged into the electrical outlets on the light posts at the site. Our Catholic lady said she would provide tables and a couple of pop-up tents for our booth, and I was in charge of getting the pies to the event on Saturday morning.

Friday night, with freezers full of ice cream plugged in on site, we put up our booth—three eight-foot tables and two rather ill-fitting tents. We'd forgotten that all the nonprofit groups in Pella had nice Dutch food carts for use at the city's annual tulip festival. As all those vendors lined up next to us along a wide sidewalk, our church tables and pop-up tents looked a little second class, but that was all we had.

My job was to transport the pies, and carting two hundred pies for fifteen miles in a church van is not easy! Vans aren't built with pie racks, and pie crust can be kind of delicate. On Saturday morning I drove as carefully as possible, damaging only a couple dozen pies. They were still edible, just not beautiful.

Arriving at the event site, I realized I had to back the van down several hundred yards of a wide sidewalk to reach our booth. It had rained hard the night before, and the ground was very soggy. I needed to stay on the sidewalk on one side to avoid driving on the soggy grass and messing up the lovely lawn. On the other side were all those handsome Pella food carts, and their owners looked nervously at me as I inched my way back to our booth. I'm not an expert at backing up a church van, but I'm happy to say that by the grace of God, I didn't hit any food carts or mar the lawn or further damage my cargo. I'm sure the effort took a couple of years off my life, though.

The event ran from 10 a.m. until 2 p.m., and the day was very hot and muggy. No one wants pie and ice cream on a hot morning, so it wasn't until about noon that we started to attract some business. I'm glad we did because that's when the transformer on our power pole exploded and caught fire. That drew attention to our booth but not the kind we wanted! The fire department came quickly to extinguish the flames, but we had no more power for our freezers, and the future of the large containers of ice cream looked grim.

Around 1 p.m. our gracious God seemed to look down on our pitiful efforts and to smile. The employees had been given "company bucks" to use for the day. We food vendors were to turn in the "company bucks" we'd collected in exchange for cash at the end of the event. But the employees had been given far more than they could spend in four hours, and by one, they started lamenting that this gift would go to waste.

That's when our Catholic lady had a brilliant idea. She climbed up on one of our tables and began shouting, "Whole pies for sale. Get your home-made pie today." People flocked to our table, so happy to have a place to spend their "company bucks" that some gave fifty dollars or more for one pie, while others bought whole containers of melting ice cream. We sold every last food item and made a profit of several thousand dollars—far more than we expected.

I've never forgotten that day, not just because it was so ridiculous in all its dimensions but because it was a good example of how God will work for good in all circumstances—and of how God blesses our crazy efforts when we are seeking to help those in need.

Get Your Priorities Right

> Hear, O Israel: The Lord is our God, the Lord alone. You shall love the Lord your God with all your heart, and with all your soul, and with all your might. Keep these words that I am commanding you today in your heart. Recite them to your children and talk about them when you are at home and when you are away, when you lie down and when you rise. (Deut. 6:4–7)

In 2001 our son, David, was a sixth-grader. He'd been saving his money for a Game Boy Advance (the latest Game Boy system at that time). By mid-July, when the Game Boy Advance was about to come out, he was checking almost daily at his favorite big box store. Finally, a clerk said, "We'll have them Wednesday." On Wednesday, David and I raced to that store and asked for the Game Boy Advance. The clerk said, "We have them, but they aren't going on sale until this weekend after we run a big ad. They'll be available at 8 a.m. Sunday."

"Eight a.m. Sunday?" we said. "We can't come then. We'll be in church." The clerk seemed moderately sympathetic and said, "Well, you could call, and maybe they'll hold one for you." So David and I formulated our plan: call the store at 8:01 a.m. on Sunday and ask them to hold a Game Boy Advance for us until shortly after noon. The plan sounded like it would work. But then David got invited out of town for the weekend, leaving with a desperate plea that I call the store Sunday morning to hold the Game Boy Advance.

Now picture this. It's Sunday, 8:01 a.m., just about time for our first worship service. The hymn sing has started in the sanctuary, and I'm dressed in my clergy robe, ready to begin worship. But at that moment I'm calling the store to hold a Game Boy Advance, and the clerk says, "I'm sorry. We can't reserve those. It's first come, first serve." My plaintive response, "But we're in church until noon," has no impact.

Bob was the preacher that day, and I'd like to say I was dutifully listening to every word of his sermon at all three worship services, but after the first one, my thoughts were more focused on how quickly I could get to the store after church. When we had shaken the last hand after worship, I told Bob, "You lock up and I'll be back. I've *got to* get that Game Boy!"

I hopped in the car, dashed to the store, ran to the electronics department, and asked for the Game Boy Advance. When the clerk said, "We're all out," I almost cried.

"You're out?" I said. "You just ran your ad this morning. How many did you have?"

The guy looked a bit embarrassed and said, "We put out six. We know we have more, but we can't find them."

"When do you expect to find them?" I rather rudely demanded.

"We don't know, lady. You could come back."

Over lunch, Bob and I discussed the Game Boy Advance crisis, and he observed, "Both you and David seem to be getting a little crazy over this." He was right. That's what our consumer culture does to us, but unwilling to give up, I said, "Well, let's go back after lunch. You have such good luck that you'll probably walk in and they'll pull one off the shelf and hand it to you." And that was exactly what happened.

The Scripture says, "Love the Lord your God with all your heart and soul and strength," not "Love your Game Boy," or whatever it was that drove me to act like I did that day. "Love the Lord your God." That's what's real in this life, and that's what we should be teaching our kids! But I'd gotten off track, and maybe you have too. I'm glad David was out of town when I tried to buy his Game Boy Advance so he didn't see the kind of parent I was at that moment. I was embarrassed about my behavior because I had allowed the things I thought were unimportant to become central in my thinking. May that never happen to you!

13

You Can't Run Away from God

> But Jonah set out to flee to Tarshish from the
> presence of the Lord. (Jonah 1:3)

In the fall of 2004, one of our Ankeny church staff members had her purse stolen from an unlocked file cabinet in her office during worship. Later that day, we learned that the Episcopal and Catholic churches in town had similar thefts. One Episcopalian had a brief conversation with the alleged thief, who gave his name and claimed he was a worship visitor. This church member gave a fairly detailed description of the man to the police and to area churches. It turned out there were warrants for his arrest elsewhere in the Des Moines metro area—all for church theft.

On a subsequent Saturday afternoon, Bob was in his church office working on his sermon. A small group was also meeting in the building with another church staff member. She reported to Bob that she had seen a man matching the thief's description enter the men's room. Not finding him there, Bob began to search the building, locating the man in the basement by the elevator in the dark.

Bob had been considering the possibility that he might run into this thief in our church and had noted the man did not appear to be violent but had been clever enough to talk his way out of previous situations. So Bob was not frightened when he encountered him by the elevator.

"Can I help you?" he asked the man.

"Oh, I'm looking for the short woman minister," he said. Asked if he meant the other staff member in the building, the man responded affirmatively.

Bob said, "I'll take you to her," and the two went upstairs. Bob called the staff member out of her meeting and escorted her and the man to the church library so the two could talk "in private." Posting another person outside the library to protect the staff member, he ran across the street to the Ankeny Police Department. The department has since moved to a new location, but in 2004 it was about a three-second run from the church.

"I've got the man you want!" Bob told the officers, and in another three seconds they ran back with him to the main church door. However, although Bob had run out that main door, it was locked from the outside, and he didn't have his keys with him. In the meantime, the man had finished asking our staff member to pray that he might find a job and was walking toward the main door to leave. Spotting the police, he turned and ran to the south door.

Bob and the police were also making their way to the unlocked south door, and the thief ran right into the arms of the law. The police asked him a few questions, which he answered untruthfully, and they arrested him, later confirming he was indeed the church thief. A member of our church who was involved in prison ministry took the opportunity to visit the thief in jail and tried to pray him into a new way of living. The incident was more proof that you shouldn't try to run away from God. Jonah learned that the hard way. Perhaps our thief could learn that lesson too.

The Paradox of Strength through Weakness

> Therefore I am content with weaknesses, insults, hardships, persecutions, and calamities for the sake of Christ; for whenever I am weak, then I am strong. (2 Cor. 12:10)

For whenever I am weak, then, through the grace of God, I am strong. In 2004, I was diagnosed with breast cancer. The hardest part of my experience was not the diagnosis, the surgery, or the radiation but the chemotherapy. It made me nauseous and I lost my hair, but worst of all, I felt totally drained. One day at the height—or the depth—of my chemotherapy, I pushed myself to go outside to see how far I could walk. I could make it only halfway down my short driveway and back. That's how I weak I was.

Nonetheless, I seldom missed work during that chemotherapy experience; I think I had to skip only one Sunday. Once or twice I had to sit down rather than stand when I preached, but I never had a problem composing my sermons. Somehow during those months, I received strength beyond my own to do what God had called me to do. I suspect you have experienced that too during times when life has laid you low. When we're too weak to carry on by ourselves, we receive strength from God.

And we usually gain wisdom along the way. Through my days of physical weakness, I gave up some of my fear of dying, I acquired a greater empathy for those dealing with life-threatening illness, and I was reminded to treasure every day because each one is a precious gift. During those times in our lives when we feel weak, when God does not seem to be restoring our strength, perhaps God's message for us is the same one Paul received: "My grace is sufficient for you, for power is made perfect in weakness" (2 Cor. 12:9).

No Storm Can Shake My Inmost Calm

> Jesus woke up and rebuked the wind, and said to the sea, "Peace! Be still!" Then the wind ceased, and there was a dead calm. (Mark 4:39)

Our faith tradition encourages music in worship not just because it is beautiful but primarily because music can put us in touch with God in a very profound way. Music is a way to open our hearts to the very heart of God, bringing strength and healing and hope. In 2004, while fighting my battle with breast cancer, I experienced that strength. The physical weakness produced by radiation treatments and chemotherapy made me feel emotionally and spiritually vulnerable.

In December 2004, Bob and I attended the high school Christmas concert. Our son, then a sophomore, was in the men's chorus. Little did I know that the performers were going to give me a great gift through the powerful words of an old hymn, "My Life Flows On," by Robert Lowry.[4] Neither Bob nor I could recall hearing this hymn before, but the beautiful musical arrangement and the powerful words brought us both to tears.

The refrain goes like this: "No storm can shake my inmost calm while to that Rock I'm clinging. Since Love is Lord of heaven and earth, how can I keep from singing?" I needed the reminder that amid the storms of life, we can find a peace that passes all understanding when we cling to Jesus. Bob and David later framed the words to that chorus as a Christmas gift. Now it daily reminds me of the strength we receive from God, stilling the storms in turbulent times. How can I keep from singing?

Why Worship?

How lovely is your dwelling place, O Lord of hosts!
My soul longs, indeed it faints for the courts of
the Lord; my heart and my flesh sing for joy to the
living God. (Ps. 84:1–2)

One summer, Bob and I attended a reunion of my family at the Lake of the Ozarks, and on Sunday morning, we sought out a nearby church for worship. It was a lovely church, well maintained inside and out. The people were exceptionally friendly, welcoming us warmly and even inviting us to an adult Sunday school class after worship. The music was excellent too, from the organist to the special selections for the day.

The problem was the sermon. I try not to be too critical of other preachers because I hope folks will be gracious in listening to my preaching. Nonetheless, I couldn't follow this preacher's point at all.

However, he had a deep, melodious voice, so I tried listening to the sermon as though it were a song with a melody I liked but with words I couldn't quite get. Fortunately, the sermon was short.

However, this preacher was fearless. Before the benediction, he walked down into the congregation and said, "Now it's time to go from this place and to be Jesus's disciples. So what was the point of the sermon today?" And he expected people to respond! A few made feeble attempts, saying things like "faith" or "service," but the honest fellow behind us said, "I have absolutely no idea." And neither did I.

Fortunately, the poor message didn't stop me from worshipping that day. You see, in worship we shift away from what we do to what God is doing, away from what is undone to what God has done, away from self to God and to other people, and away from an uncertain future to a solid hope. Worship reorients and recenters our lives.

Here's how such worship happened for me that day. My life was refocused not by the sermon or the prayers but by a hymn after the sermon. Through that song, God met me right at the point of my need. We'd been at a reunion with my two brothers, their children, and grandchildren. This was the first time we had all been together since my father's funeral. It had been great watching my brothers' grandchildren jumping off the dock into the lake just like we had done as kids.

But in worship as I sang the closing hymn, the passage of time hit me over the head. I was at the point in my life when I had more years behind me than ahead of me, and the tears began to flow down my cheeks. *Slow down, life!* was my inner cry, and that's where God met me through the hymn, saying, "Fear not! I am with you always—today and tomorrow and the next day. Times may change, but I am constant, and I am with you." That was just the refocus I needed to draw me out of my self-perspective to a broader vision of God's purposes.

So here's the promise. When you are open to it, God will meet you as you worship and will refocus your life toward discipleship and service, and you will go forth knowing the hope and the purpose found in loving God with all your heart and mind and soul and strength.

CHAPTER 2

Lessons in Loving

Enduring Love

> Love bears all things, believes all things, hopes all things, endures all things. (1 Cor. 13:7)

When I consider the phrase "Love endures all things," the person who comes immediately to mind is my paternal grandmother, Edith Dalton. She did not have an easy life. As a young mother during the Great Depression, she stayed in Kansas with her two sons while my grandfather, Orville Dalton, went to find work wherever he could. Then came this headline in a Wichita, Kansas, newspaper: "A Long Ride in Ambulance." The story, dated February 23, 1933, said, "O.R. Dalton, 40-year-old Wichita oil driller, was in the Veterans Hospital here today after a 400-mile ride in an ambulance from Pampa, Texas, where his backbone was crushed in a traffic accident. His condition was described as dangerous."

My grandfather spent almost two years in the hospital; he would never walk again; he would never work again. In the midst of the Depression, my grandmother got a full-time job and life went on, but it wasn't easy to raise two children, take care of an invalid husband, and support the family. Grandma worked as a saleswoman in ladies' wear at a downtown department store in Wichita. She didn't drive, so every morning she would pack her sack lunch and walk to the bus stop for work, and every night she would ride the bus home and fix dinner for my grandfather. Although I remember my grandfather with great fondness since he was often our babysitter, his disability must have made life hard for my grandmother.

When my brothers and I were young, if we were lucky, on Friday Grandma would invite us to spend the night. We would sleep on the fold-out bed in the living room, and on Saturday we would help her with the wonderful baking she enjoyed but had so little time to do. Each Sunday morning, Grandma would walk over to the neighborhood Methodist church, and on Sunday evening, she'd have the whole family over for a delicious dinner.

When I was a child, no downtown shopping excursion was complete without a trip to see Grandma at the department store. She worked there until her retirement, even as her back became bowed with osteoporosis and her ankles became thick from constant standing. Every Christmas, we knew our gifts from Grandma would come from Walker's Department Store, carefully picked out when special sales and her employee discount guaranteed the best bargain.

As an adult, I learned more about Grandma through her devotional book, *Abundant Living*, by E. Stanley Jones. It was given to me after her death. Thumbing through the pages of this book, I saw that my grandmother was an underliner, and from her underlinings, I gained wonderful insights into her life and her faith. Grandma consistently underlined things like this: "In quietness and confidence shall be my strength"; "Go out each day and do some positive good to the person against whom you hold resentments." This is one of my favorites: "Life is bound to kick you, for all get knocks—some more, some less—the important thing is the direction in which you are kicked. Make life kick you forward!"[1]

I'm sure my grandmother's life was hard; she never made much money; she never got a promotion; she was sometimes very tired. But that's not what I remember about her. What I remember is her enduring love and her caring spirit. After her death in 1982, someone sent my father a sympathy card that said, "You know, we always called Mrs. Dalton the Madonna of Lady's Wear." And so she was—a woman of God's love. Sometimes the work we do may not seem very important, but that isn't what counts. It is the love that endures.

Grandmothers: My First Mentors

> I am reminded of your sincere faith, a faith that lived first in your grandmother Lois and your mother Eunice and now, I am sure, lives in you. For this reason I remind you to rekindle the gift of God that is within you through the laying on of my hands; for God did not give us a spirit of cowardice, but rather a spirit of power and of love and of self-discipline. (2 Tim. 1:5–7)

The prominent early mentors in my life were my two grandmothers. I often tell the story of Grandma Dalton, who triumphed over very difficult circumstances with a gracious, loving spirit. But I was also blessed by my maternal grandmother, Mamo to us.

I grew up in what was surely a child's paradise. My family lived in a duplex with my parents, my brothers, and me on one side and with my Krehbiel grandparents, Mamo and Papo, on the other side. So, no matter how much trouble I got into on my side of the duplex, I knew I would always find unconditional love and acceptance on my grandparents' side of the house.

Mamo was one of those people who never had a bad thing to say about anyone. Kindness seemed to ooze from her pores. She was always giving. In fact, if you admired any of her possessions, she would always try to give it to you.

In their retirement, Mamo and Papo owned and operated several small businesses in the Lake of the Ozarks area in Missouri. One of them, a gift shop near Bagnall Dam, consistently lost money because my grandmother turned it into her personal social service agency to help out employees going through hard times. I think they sometimes took advantage of her, but she never held it against them. She was always there for them, kind of like God is always there for us. She too is a model of God's love for me.

I Want to Love Like That

> So he [the Prodigal Son] set off and went to his father. But while he was still far off, his father saw him and was filled with compassion; he ran and put his arms around him and kissed him. (Luke 15:20)

When I was in the fourth grade, my grandfather Krehbiel (Papo) became ill while traveling in southern California. Since he needed to be hospitalized for several weeks, my grandmother asked Mom to help out. Although school was still in session, my mother loaded my two brothers and me on a train and took us along to California, while Dad stayed in Wichita, Kansas, to work. We spent several weeks in California, and in between trips to the hospital, we visited Disneyland, Knott's Berry Farm, and the ocean. While it may not have been great fun for Mom, the trip was a treat for us kids. When Papo recovered enough to travel, my grandparents flew home to Kansas and Mom drove us back in their car. On our way, we spent the night at the Grand Canyon in Arizona.

During our short stay in a cabin near the canyon rim, Mom let us play outside on our own. We had strict instructions not to venture far away and definitely not to go down any paths into the canyon itself. My brothers, ages eleven and seven, found the temptation to explore too great to resist and set off down one of the narrow canyon paths. I thought they were foolish to disobey, and like a typical ten-year-old sibling, I hoped they would get in a lot of trouble with Mom. After some time, Mom came to check on us. "Where are your brothers?" she asked.

"Well, they did just what you told them not to do," I said, and pointed out the path they had taken.

Mom's face became pale, and she quickly made her way down the narrow path, shouting, "Bobby! Johnny!" Fortunately, just then they reappeared, looking rather tired and thirsty from their escapade. *Now they are going to get it!* I thought gleefully. But to my surprise, my mother scooped them up in her arms and hugged them, with tears streaming down her face. Jesus's parable of the prodigal son reminds us that this is how God loves us, even when we travel down the wrong path. I want to love like that.

Just Love

> Above all, clothe yourselves with love, which binds everything together in perfect harmony. (Col. 3:14)

In the months before our son, David, was born, the church where we were serving had a baby shower for us. Since our parents lived outside of Iowa and couldn't come, the congregation invited them to write us letters giving us advice—pearls of wisdom—on child-raising. I'll never forget what my father wrote.

My dad believed he was always right. I didn't always agree with what he said; sometimes I was sure he was wrong, but that didn't matter. It was "Father Knows Best" at our house. So I wasn't surprised when the letter of advice he sent was a long list of suggestions—probably twenty or so—on parenting.

But what was surprising was that one by one, he had crossed out each of those wise suggestions, and at the end he simply wrote, "Just love your child as much as your mom and I love you kids, and you'll do just fine." Just love. Pretty good advice.

Heroes

> Therefore, since we are surrounded by so great a cloud of witnesses, let us also lay aside every weight and the sin that clings so closely, and let us run with perseverance the race that is set before us. (Heb. 12:1)

The song "Wind Beneath My Wings"[2] was sung at the funeral for my sister-in-law, Leslie Dalton, who died of cancer at forty. A line in the song says, "Did I ever tell you you're my hero?" That's a powerful image because we need heroes. A Christian writer, Mary Lou Redding, defines a hero like this: "Heroes are those who turn our lives, who cause us to be more than we might be otherwise—stronger, wiser, more tender, more authentic."[3]

Leslie was that kind of a hero for me, but more important she was a hero to my brother, to her two young daughters, and to the children's choir she directed at her church. At her funeral, the minister said one of the hardest things he had to do was meet with those children and explain to them why Leslie, who had directed them just the week before, would not be with them anymore.

I spent several days with my brother and my nieces after Leslie's funeral. I took a walk with my niece Emily, who was then twelve. She told me her mom had often said that as her girls grew older and were off doing things on their own, she would worry when she wasn't with them. "Now," Emily said with wisdom beyond her years, "I guess she can be with me wherever I am." That's how it is with that "cloud of witnesses"—those heroes in our lives who have gone on before us. They are with us, cheering us on in this race called life, and there is great strength in that.

Self-giving Love

> We know love by this, that he laid down his life
> for us—and we ought to lay down our lives for one
> another. (1 John 3:16)

In my 2009 Labor Day sermon, I gave thanks for the wonderful
lady who was a special gift to our family. As a young woman of
twenty, Yvonne started cleaning house for my parents one day a
week. I was a toddler at the time. Over the years she also worked for
my grandparents, who lived next door, and for family friends who
lived down the street, so I saw Yvonne several times a week while I
was growing up. I never knew much about her family because she
lived in another part of town, but she knew everything about our
family—and she loved us in spite of that. My mother had many close
friends, but when I asked her once who her best friend was, she said
instantly, "Oh, Yvonne. I couldn't live without her."

Over the years, the truth of that statement became clear. When
my parents had to dispose of some of my grandparents' property
in Missouri, Yvonne went along to help them. When they moved
to a smaller house, Yvonne helped them pack. After my mother
suffered two debilitating strokes, Yvonne began working in my
parents' home several hours every day, becoming my mother's home
health aide. Ultimately, Yvonne came daily to take care of my dad
through his final illness. My proud, stubborn father didn't want his
kids sitting around his bedside as he was dying, so it was Yvonne
who had to make the call to say, "Martha, your dad is gone." As
I was preparing to sell my parents' home, Yvonne kept an eye on
things when I couldn't be in Wichita. For more than fifty years, this
quiet little lady held the members of my family together, and I am
extremely grateful. She loved us more than we ever deserved! This
type of everyday caring—self-giving love for others—is what makes
a difference in God's eyes.

Goodness Embodied

> Finally, beloved, whatever is true, whatever is honorable, whatever is just, whatever is pure, whatever is pleasing, whatever is commendable, if there is any excellence and if there is anything worthy of praise, think about these things. Keep on doing the things that you have learned and received and heard and seen in me, and the God of peace will be with you. (Phil. 4:8–9)

I've been blessed to know many wonderful Christian people, but near the top of my list of Christlike people will always be Bob's great-aunt, Margaret Barnett (Marmie), who died at one hundred. She's the Ward family saint.

Marmie was never married. She had several proposals, but she felt a stronger obligation to raise the two children of her widowed older brother, Burney. His wife died when their children, Henry and Mayme Pearl (Bob's mom), were ten and five years old, respectively.

Marmie became a first-grade teacher and then the supervisor of all the first-grade teachers in Kansas City, Missouri. She was a Sunday school teacher and a visitor to shut-ins. She didn't have that one close relationship of marriage, but in its place, she had a deep impact on dozens of lives. I don't know if she ever regretted not marrying, but I know few people who lived happier, richer lives.

When he was in fifth grade, our son, David, had to write an essay about a personal hero. He chose his great-great-aunt Marmie. Here's just one example of what made all of us admire her so greatly. In the fifties in Kansas City, the schools were still segregated. White children were taught in predominantly white schools by white teachers; African American children were taught in predominantly black schools by African American teachers. Marmie supervised all the first-grade teachers, both white and black.

One day, while Marmie was visiting one of the African American schools, lunch hour arrived. The school principal prepared a lunch tray for her and placed it in an office so she could eat by herself, on the understanding that whites and blacks did not sit down to eat together.

Telling the story, Marmie said, "Well, that didn't make any sense to me because I was there to help them, and how could I help them if I didn't get to know them?" In that spirit, she picked up her tray and brought it into the teachers' lunchroom. For a few moments, there was a nervous silence as Marmie sat down by the first-grade teachers, but soon they were all laughing and talking together. Marmie said that was the last time they ever considered giving her a private lunch.

How is it that some people seem to have such innate goodness? They appear to know instinctively how to do the right thing all the time. For Marmie, this knowledge was deeply rooted in her Christian faith. Perhaps that's why Philippians 4:8–9 was her favorite passage of Scripture!

On Being a Friend

> When Jesus returned to Capernaum after some days, it was reported that he was at home. So many gathered around that there was no longer room for them, not even in front of the door; and he was speaking the word to them. Then some people came, bringing to him a paralyzed man, carried by four of them. And when they could not bring him to Jesus because of the crowd, they removed the roof above him; and after having dug through it, they let down the mat on which the paralytic lay. When Jesus saw their faith, he said to the paralytic, "Son, your sins are forgiven." (Mark 2:1–5)

Compassion invites us to enter into another's pain, and kindness requires us to act for the good of another. We don't automatically do these things. We need to decide each day to act for the good of others—to be like the people who lowered the paralyzed man through the roof in hopes that Jesus would heal him. Sometimes acting with compassion isn't easy. I remember a time when I had to choose whether to be a friend.

During my brief time as a social worker (1972–76), a teenage girl named Kathie was admitted to the hospital where I worked. She had taken a drug overdose—a suicide attempt, they said. I was asked to visit her to offer counseling and referral. A nurse told me that Kathie's mother had died when the girl was about ten and that her father was an alcoholic judged by the courts as unfit to parent. She'd been in and out of foster homes for some time.

When I first called on this young patient, she would barely look me in the eye. But I kept coming back. After a few days she raised her eyes to look at me; a few days later she began to talk. Kathie saw little purpose to her life; she didn't belong anywhere and wondered who needed her. She'd been assigned a psychiatrist who had prescribed various pills, and so she'd taken them—all at once. The more we visited, the more I thought, *This young girl doesn't need a counselor. She needs a friend. Maybe God wants that friend to be me.*

Becoming involved in Kathie's life meant confronting the mental health workers who had written her off as seriously disturbed. It meant checking in with the school personnel who thought she didn't care. Soon Kathie was back in high school and working part time at our hospital. She would often stop by my office just to check in. She was doing well. After Bob and I had left for seminary, we exchanged lots of letters with Kathie; a high school graduation announcement was followed by college grade reports. After all, if you haven't got a mom or a dad, you need somebody to say "Good work" when you bring home those As and Bs.

Upon returning to Iowa, we had a wonderful reunion with Kathie. We shared the ups and downs of her life, her graduation from college, and her first job. She joined the smaller church we were serving and volunteered with the youth program. She was on her way to a healthy, happy life when she was killed at age twenty-five in an automobile accident.

Rear-ended by a car traveling at high speed, her car burst into flame. Kathie died instantly, and everything in her car was destroyed except for her purse, which contained her address book. In it, she had carefully recorded all her acquaintances and their relationships to her—classmate, fellow employee, former foster family. I came to our names. The entry didn't say "Martha Ward, social worker, pastor." It simply said "Bob and Martha Ward—best friends." We were blessed to be friends who helped Kathie know the healing power of love. And she showed us how compassion and kindness are contagious. Once you share those with another, they multiply and come right back to you!

We Are Set Free to Serve

> Be subject to one another out of reverence for Christ. (Eph. 5:21–22)

In June 1983 when Bob and I began to serve as co-pastors, a local television station did a "close-up" segment on our team ministry for the evening news. It is always exciting and a little scary to be on the news, but one of the most interesting things about such a close-up is the feedback you get. Judging from the reaction we received, the most important aspect of our team seemed to be the fact that Bob did half the housework (or perhaps more than half, as rumor has it).

The issue of who did the dishes or the laundry was not central to our theology or to our ministry. But it was important because of what it said about the servant role. Doing the laundry is a servant role in a household. It is not a prestige job but something someone does on behalf of the family. It was an example of a servant role Bob had chosen—a choice he could make because he had said, "I will not be bound by sex-role stereotypes that say men don't share equally in household tasks. I will be free to serve."

Genuine Love

> Love one another with mutual affection; outdo one another in showing honor. (Rom. 12:10)

In 2011, Bob and I took a two-week trip to the southeastern United States, traveling as far as Charleston, South Carolina. On our way back to Iowa, we stopped at a small restaurant in Tennessee for a late-night piece of pie. As we ate, we chatted with the young employee, probably high school age, who was cleaning up for the night.

"Where are you from?" he asked.

"Iowa," we said.

"Well, where have you been?"

"South Carolina," we said.

"Driving—in a car?" he asked, and when we said yes, he said, "Wow, you must love each other a lot."

"Well, we used to," Bob replied with a grin.

CHAPTER 3

Christ in Our Midst

Help in Changing Directions

> Now as he was going along and approaching
> Damascus, suddenly a light from heaven flashed
> around him. He fell to the ground and heard a voice
> saying to him, "Saul, Saul, why do you persecute
> me?" He asked, "Who are you, Lord?" The reply
> came, "I am Jesus, whom you are persecuting. But
> get up and enter the city, and you will be told what
> you are to do." (Acts 9:3–6)

Have you ever found yourself going in the wrong direction?
Bob's great-grandfather, William Henry Ward, was a captain in the
Civil War, and Bob's family preserved about twenty of the captain's
letters from that war. The captain's letter of July 19, 1862, written
from his regiment's camp in Greenbrier County, Virginia, recounts
how he and another officer became separated from the regiment, the
47th Ohio Volunteer Infantry. While trying to catch up with their
troops, they came to a fork in the road and could not tell which way
the Union soldiers had gone. They were in Confederate territory, and
Bob's great-grandfather wrote, "As ill luck would have it, we took

the wrong road, and the inhabitants, having a special dislike to blue uniforms, would tell us nothing."

There they were, inadvertently on a risky road in enemy territory. Maybe you've inadvertently found yourself on a risky path. I think Christ intervened for Bob's great-grandfather when he and his fellow officer found themselves in this difficult situation.

The captain's letter continued:

> We had penetrated nearly twenty miles farther into the enemy's country than our forces had yet been, when accidently meeting a Union man (I supposed him to be), he warned us that we were within four miles of a camp of rebel cavalry and advised us to retrace our steps. Thinking he might be trying to trap us, we made light of his advice and bidding him "Good evening," we pushed on toward the rebel camp. But soon coming to a dense woods, we turned off the road, secreted our horses in a swamp and stood guard alternately until well after midnight. Then we retraced our steps, reaching our regiment by daylight. Our appearance created quite a joyful surprise in our regiment as the whole command had given us up as dead or as being prisoners on our way to Richmond."[1]

Now isn't that interesting? Twenty miles into enemy territory, they meet an unknown Union man who just happens to be walking down that road and who says, "Turn around. You're going the wrong way." Maybe that was just coincidental, or maybe Christ appeared through that unknown man to put them on the right road. They weren't exactly sure about this encounter, so they hid in the woods for a while, but then they followed the messenger's advice and got to safety.

Most of us will not experience Christ's presence the way Paul did, as a blinding light that knocks us off our feet. Christ is likelier to appear in subtler guises—in all those coincidences that make us wonder as we look back on them, in the persistent nudges to our consciences when we've gone astray, in doors opening to new possibilities when we're at a dead end, or through a friend, a coach, or a guide suddenly walking alongside of us when it appears we've lost our way. Perhaps you've had such experiences. I know I have, and I've come to identify them as gifts from Christ.

The Roadblocks Are Removed

> And suddenly there was a great earthquake; for an angel of the Lord, descending from heaven, came and rolled back the stone and sat on it. His appearance was like lightning, and his clothing white as snow. For fear of him the guards shook and became like dead men. But the angel said to the women, "Do not be afraid; I know that you are looking for Jesus who was crucified. He is not here; for he has been raised, as he said. Come, see the place where he lay. (Matt. 28:2–6)

Most of us have faced roadblocks in our lives. If there is only one way to reach your destination, if you're stuck, or if you're trapped by the barricade, this can be a very serious problem. I remember one such time in my life.

In 1964, as a junior in high school, I was part of a summer student tour of Germany. The most moving experience of that trip was my first view of the Berlin Wall. Erected in 1961, it didn't fall until 1989. I will never forget how viewing it made me give thanks for my freedom. Seeing the wall—brick upon brick, with barbed wire strung across the top and guards on patrol—I realized for the first time that some people in our world were not free. We could enter East Berlin as tourists, but the people of East Berlin could not pass through that roadblock to the West.

We did not enter East Berlin as part of the regular tour but had the option to visit in small, unsupervised groups. So a friend and I made our way through the wall by an entry point known as Checkpoint Charlie. We spent an afternoon sightseeing in the museums, shops, and restaurants of East Berlin and then decided to return to West Berlin by subway.

That's when we ran into a roadblock. We reached the wall and the subway stopped, but a guard at the exit, speaking rapidly in German, refused to let us get off. For two American high school girls, this was a very scary moment. In a divided city, in a dingy subway station, we struggled with our limited German to understand why we were being detained. In what was probably five minutes but seemed like hours, we came to understand that we had to leave East Berlin the same way we entered. We were directed back to Checkpoint Charlie where we were permitted to exit.

In this wandering journey of our lives, we seldom exit a situation at the same place we entered it. We all hit those roadblocks—the exterior roadblocks that keep us from getting where we need to be and the interior barriers that can keep us from becoming the people God intends for us to be.

Matthew paints a dramatic picture of the stone—a roadblock—being rolled away from the tomb on Easter morning. Christ had risen! Easter is a powerful reminder that we don't have to be the same old way we have always been. The risen Christ can turn any roadblock into a road to wholeness. That's because the resurrection isn't just a miracle that happened two thousand years ago. Just as the Berlin Wall fell in 1989, so the risen Christ continues to remove roadblocks to new possibilities in our lives and in our world today.

Who Is Jesus to You?

Now when Jesus came into the district of Caesarea Philippi, he asked his disciples, "Who do people say that the Son of Man is?" And they said, "Some say John the Baptist, but others Elijah, and still others Jeremiah or one of the prophets." He said to them, "But who do you say that I am?" Simon Peter answered, "You are the Messiah, the Son of the living God." (Matt. 16:13–16)

One evening during my junior year in college, I had a theological discussion with a roommate. I wouldn't have called it that at the time. I would have said we were talking about our religious beliefs. I had been raised in the Methodist Church; as a college student, I dutifully got up on Sunday mornings and went to church in my college town, and I volunteered to help with the church's youth group during the week. I liked church; I was no stranger to the Christian faith.

But in this discussion—one of those times when I was trying to be honest about my beliefs—I said to my roommate, "I believe in God and know God loves me. But I just don't know what I believe about Jesus. Was he really the Son of God? Did he really rise from the dead?" My roommate, a faithful Christian herself, looked absolutely shocked, as if I had said something terrible. "Oh, Martha, you must never say that!" she told me. "How can you be a Christian and not know what you believe about Jesus?"

That was a conversation stopper—we never returned to that topic as roommates. But I often thought about this discussion. In fact, it was probably one of the most important conversations of my young adult life because it started me on a lifelong journey into deeper relationship with Jesus. "Who is Jesus Christ? What do his life, death, and resurrection mean to my life?" Those were active questions that led my seeking for years to come, bringing me to the place where, as a mature adult, I could say Jesus Christ is my Lord and Savior. Through my lived experience, I know Christ is alive and present in our world.

The Cleansing Power of Christ

> A leper came to him begging him, and kneeling he said to him, "If you choose, you can make me clean." Moved with pity, Jesus stretched out his hand and touched him, and said to him, "I do choose. Be made clean!" Immediately the leprosy left him, and he was made clean. (Mark 1:40–42)

"If you choose, you can make me clean." I remember when a cry for help like that first came to me. In the 1970s while doing hospital social work, the hospital administrator notified me that I had been selected to serve as a sponsor of a support group for persons who admitted to abusing their children. My leadership was part of the hospital's commitment to community involvement. I was a naive young do-gooder, and while glad to serve in this role, I was nervous about it. I thought child abusers were bad people. Further I knew this kind of abuse was passed on in a cycle from one generation to the next, so the situation had a certain hopelessness to it. What difference could I or this group possibly make?

People with child abuse problems can come from any walk of life or income range, but the persons in this group were low-income folks who had lived hard lives, many being abused themselves. They were tough, rough-speaking women who didn't hesitate to tell you what they thought of you. Initially, they didn't think much of me, and I was scared of them and of what they had done to their kids.

However, I was profoundly moved when one group member told her story. "I found myself gripping my young daughter's shoulders," the woman said, "pounding her head on the floor, crying, 'I love you! I don't want to hurt you!' over and over again until I heard her crying softly, 'Mommy, I love you too.' What was I doing to this child I had wanted so badly?" Her experience reminded me that these were not hardened, angry, vicious people but scared, isolated, discouraged parents who had perhaps never been touched in a loving and healing way.

We met weekly for several years, and during those years I was sometimes called to be an advocate for group members. Bit by bit, they shared their stories with me and the other co-sponsor of our group and came to trust us because we didn't desert them. We dared to give them hugs and signs of encouragement when they made good parenting choices. Nonetheless, while they were making strides to break the cycle of abuse, the fact that they had at one time committed child abuse—plus the reality that they were generally welfare moms—created a stigma that was hard to overcome. Sometimes I would accompany them to the welfare office, the police department, the courthouse, or even the doctor's office just to remind those usually fair professionals that these struggling mothers were human too and deserved proper treatment.

I learned a lot from my experience with that group. For example, when we reach out with love to those who have been cast out or stigmatized by society, God can use us to change lives. It's been many years since I worked with that group, but I have occasionally run into one of the participants and have been able to follow the lives of her children a bit. They grew up to become healthy and happy adults, thanks to the fact that she received acceptance and love when she was going through the hard times of her young adulthood. I also observed that this mom became an active member of her local church. Rejected no more, now a contributing part of her church community, she was using her strong faith to encourage others.

Christ Lifts Our Burdens

> Jesus said, "Come to me, all you that are weary and are carrying heavy burdens, and I will give you rest. Take my yoke upon you, and learn from me; for I am gentle and humble in heart, and you will

find rest for your souls. For my yoke is easy, and my burden is light." (Matt. 11:28–30)

Bob and I took our first backpacking trip when we were in our twenties. We were vacationing in Glacier National Park and decided to try an overnight backpack experience. While we had never backpacked before, we couldn't imagine there was anything we needed to learn about it. We purchased cheap backpacks at a discount store and loaded them up with our "lightweight" camping equipment.

For our inaugural backpack, we chose a beautiful trail that gradually ascended onto a mountain through alpine meadows and across babbling brooks. The hike was marvelous except for the backpacks. Because we hadn't done any training, walking while carrying so much weight on our shoulders was hard and painful. We were sore and exhausted when we reached our designated camping spot in the late afternoon. Wilderness camping areas in national parks usually have several camp sites, so when we arrived at our area, we had neighbors—two friendly young men who came over to greet us. "You're new to backpacking, aren't you?" one of them said. (*How could it be so obvious?* we wondered.)

"We can tell by the way you're carrying your packs. You don't have any hip belts," he said. (Since our inexpensive packs came with no hip belts, we had devised small waist straps to hold them in place.) "You're not supposed to carry your pack solely on your shoulders. A good hip belt will transfer much of the weight to the rest of your body. It's a wonder you made it up here at all." These two fellows turned out to be owners of a backpacking store and experts on backpacking, and over our shared supper that night, they taught us a lot.

It was almost as if God had sent a couple of angels to keep an eye on these two foolish children. We were glad to be with our new friends, because in the morning, as we prepared to break camp, it began to rain heavily. "Where are you heading?" one of them shouted over the pounding rain. "Back down to the valley," we said, and he asked, "How about us going with you?" (Isn't it wonderful how God seems to know when you might need extra help?) They taught us a lot that day about making a descent on wet, slippery rock paths. One of them led the way, while the other brought up the rear, and we were grateful they were there.

I was especially glad when we got to a point where the path crossed a narrow stream bubbling its way down the mountain. It was still raining heavily. The stream wasn't very deep, but the bottom was rocky and the water was moving swiftly. Worst of all, the bridge across it was nothing more than a solitary log—round, wet, and slippery! (It was probably no more than six feet long, but it seemed a mile long to me.)

Our backpacking leader made his way across the log, followed by Bob, but when it was my turn, I froze. I was sure there was no way I could make it across that slippery log, carrying my heavy pack, without falling into the stream. At best, I would wind up completely soaked or would be injured; at worst, I would be swept down the mountain in the rush of the water.

Then a voice behind me gently said, "Here, let me carry your pack. Then you can either walk or crawl across the log. You can do it." Suddenly the burden on my shoulders was gone, and I got down on my hands and knees and inched my way across the log. When I was safely across, the seasoned backpacker in the rear picked up my pack while wearing his and nimbly walked across the log. And he didn't make fun of my fear or awkwardness in any way.

"Here, let me carry your pack, your burden, your baggage," says our Lord, "whatever weighs you down and makes you think you cannot face the challenges that lie ahead. Let me lighten your load so you can move ahead, and if it's too scary to walk, it's okay to crawl. I will see you safely across." Christ doesn't just show you how to transfer the weight of what you are carrying from your shoulders to your whole body; he transfers it to his body so you can travel light.

Jesus Quenches Our Life Thirst

> Jesus said to her, "Everyone who drinks of this water will be thirsty again, but those who drink of the water that I will give them will never be thirsty. The water that I will give will become in them a spring of water gushing up to eternal life." (John 4:13–14)

Have you ever been really thirsty? I remember being in that condition on a backpacking trip Bob and I took a number of years ago. We were hiking and camping with friends in the Selway-Bitterroot National Wilderness in Idaho. It's a beautiful area but rather dry, so it's important to stay near streams and rivers for water. We had been backpacking for two days and were having a wonderful time—so wonderful we decided to become even more adventuresome.

Rather than taking the route marked out by the ranger, we studied our topographical map, found what looked like an interesting path, and set out to follow it. It wasn't until several hours later, after our path seemed to gradually disappear, that we again studied our map. We then realized we hadn't been following a designated path at all but the line indicating the boundary of the wilderness area. Generally, when you realize you have been following the wrong path, you can turn around and go back. But when you have been following no path at all, it's hard to retrace your steps! So we decided to forge ahead, which meant climbing a rather steep hill.

"Once we get to the top of this hill," we told each other, "we'll be able to see where we are, and we'll know which direction to take." This was a good idea except the hill we were climbing was very high. Every time we thought we were at the top, we would discover that we had simply reached a ridge and that the hill still unfolded above us. That would not have been so bad except that evening was rolling around, and we were about to run out of water. For some reason, knowing you are nearly out of water makes you even thirstier. We were rationing our water in sips, and it never seemed to quench our thirst.

As night fell, we decided we must stop our ascent. We began the difficult process of figuring out how to pitch camp and to sleep on a hillside. We decided to skip dinner (we had no choice since all our food was freeze dried and required water) and found an animal path almost wide enough to pitch our tent. We tied the tent to several trees so we wouldn't roll down the hill in our sleep and spent a very uncomfortable night.

In the morning we realized we had some food that was not freeze dried. The beef jerky strips might have helped our hunger, but they were very salty. Eating them would only make us thirstier, and we were already rationing our water. So on we went, climbing upward. The sun got hotter and hotter, and we became thirstier and thirstier. At one point Bob threw himself exhausted on the ground and said, "You'll just have to go one without me!" I said, "I'm not going any farther if you aren't," but our two friends had the wisdom to coax us into moving on.

Finally, we reached the top of the hill, regained our bearings, and began to trudge in what we hoped was the right direction. Thirsty and exhausted, we at least had renewed hope. Then, rounding a bend, we saw a most glorious sight—a little spring of water trickling out of the rocks. We hoped it wasn't a hallucination! We sat by that spring for a long time, filling our cups and drinking again and again. Water never tasted so good!

I think Jesus was especially thirsty when he stopped at the well in Samaria. He must have been to ask a Samaritan woman for a drink. After all, Jews were foreigners in Samaria, Samaritans and Jews were enemies, and no proper Jewish man would ever talk to a strange woman in public. I think the Samaritan woman must have been thirsty too. The fact that she was alone at the well at noontime tells us something about this woman; perhaps she was an outcast, not accepted by the other women who came to the well for water each morning. She was thirsty for more than water!

When we were lost in Selway-Bitterroot, we knew we were thirsty. Sometimes, however, when we human beings are lost in the wilderness of everyday living, we may not recognize our longing for acceptance, for purpose, for meaning. Like the woman at the well, we are among the thirsty. And just as Jesus came to her, Christ comes to us, offering living water. Whenever I think of that life-giving spring in Selway-Bitterroot, I remember Jesus's words to the Samaritan woman: "The water that I will give will become in them a spring of water gushing up to eternal life."

Adrift

> Jesus said, "I have come as light into the world, so that everyone who believes in me should not remain in the darkness." (John 12:46)

In 1988 Bob and I spent the Fourth of July weekend with my family at the Lake of the Ozarks in Missouri. On Saturday, July 2, my younger brother, John, suggested we go by boat to watch the large fireworks display being put on by businesses in the area.

As night was falling, we piled into John's boat. To provide an anchor while we watched the display, John tied a large rock to a long rope on the boat, and off we went. When we reached an ideal viewing spot, my older brother, Bob, threw out our makeshift anchor, and we watched it slip from the rope and head for the bottom of the lake. *So much for an anchor!* we thought. *We'll pay attention to where we are floating and avoid other boats in the area.*

The fireworks began, and to get a good view, John would periodically turn off our boat lights, allowing us to watch in as much darkness as possible. Suddenly, out of the night, another boat sped right up to us. John flipped on the lights and shouted, "Hey! Watch out!" Then we realized it was the lake patrol, the police on water.

"Are you aware that you've been sitting out in the middle of a busy lake channel at night with no lights on?" one of the officers asked. "We've been observing you for some time. May we please see some identification and your boat registration?" Naturally John had left without identification, but luckily, he had his boat registration. Yes, he was aware the lights were off.

"Do you have an anchor or are you just drifting?" was the next question. And sheepishly we had to answer that we were just drifting. They did not care that we had lost our makeshift anchor. After a short lecture on water safety, they gave us a ticket for "being adrift with no visible means of illumination" and sent us on our way.

"Adrift with no visible means of illumination." We hadn't thought we had created a hazard for ourselves or others, but apparently we had. I wonder if that is also true of the way we sometimes lead our lives—adrift with no visible means of illumination, unknowingly presenting a hazard to ourselves and others. Life need not be that way. Christ stands ready to illuminate our life journeys while anchoring us to the firm foundation of God's love.

Incarnation

> Look the virgin shall conceive and bear a son, and they shall name him Emmanuel, which means "God is with us." (Matt. 1:23)

The most powerful Christmas Eve of my life occurred in 1989. Bob and I were serving Grace United Methodist Church in Waterloo, Iowa, when we were drawn into an interesting Christmas Eve tradition. I can't say we wanted to do it at first. Our church was located one block from the county jail, which was usually full. The jail has since been remodeled, but in 1989 it was a classic urban lockup—large cellblocks holding multiple prisoners, with bars separating the cells from the walkway used by guards and visitors. One year, a member of a church in neighboring Cedar Falls contacted us, saying, "We have a group going caroling at the county jail after our Christmas Eve service, and since the jail is just down the street from your church, we wondered if you and some folks from your church would like to come along."

No, I thought. *I wouldn't like to do that.* I wanted to conclude Christmas Eve with candlelight and "Silent Night" in the sanctuary. I didn't want to end it with the clanking of steel doors unlocking jailhouse corridors and with bright lights glaring on institutional green walls. But then that familiar phrase "What would Jesus do?" ran through my head, and I said, "Sure, we'll come."

Next the person asked, "Could you also chip in some money the jailer can give the prisoners so they can buy extra treats at the jail canteen for Christmas?"

"Oh, sure," I said, thinking, *Great, we have to go sing and pay for it too. Bah humbug.* But we found funds in the mission account, gathered a group of carolers, and off we went to the county jail following Christmas Eve worship that year—and every year thereafter as long as we served in Waterloo.

That first year we took our son, David, with us. He was just a toddler, and we carried him as we walked from cellblock to cellblock singing carols. At each stop, most inmates would smile and sing along or wipe away an occasional tear. As we sang, David became restless in our arms and wanted to get down. Reluctantly we let him down in front of us, and immediately he toddled up to a jail cell and grabbed the bars. As he did, the inmates reached out to touch him. At first, that made me very nervous, and then I realized what was happening.

This little child in their midst reminded them of the baby Jesus. They wanted reach through the bars of their imprisonment to connect with Jesus. The longing to connect with Jesus is at the very heart of Christmas. Perhaps that's why God chose to come to us as a vulnerable baby. Everyone loves a baby, and we want to connect! And here's the good news. God incarnate in Jesus Christ wants to connect with us. Whether the bars of our imprisonment are visible or are buried deep within our souls, our incarnate God reaches out to us in love.

Saying Yes to Christ

> As surely as God is faithful, our word to you has not been "Yes and No." For the Son of God, Jesus Christ, whom we proclaimed among you, Silvanus and Timothy and I, was not "Yes and No"; but in him it is always "Yes." For in him every one of God's promises is a "Yes." (2 Cor. 1:18–20)

At one and a half, our son, David, had quite a vocabulary. He quickly managed *no*, generally repeating it twice for emphasis—"no, no." If we said, "David, would you like to take a nap?" or "David, would you like to eat this nice spinach?" he would likely say, "No, no." Interestingly enough, he had not yet learned to say yes.

And maybe that's true of us in relationship to God. In Christ, God is always inviting us to say yes to a closer, deeper relationship, but too often we say no. That divine presence might cause us to change, and change makes us nervous, so we often say no, no to the divine offer. Christ never forces his way into our hearts. Rather, Christ is available but waits for us to extend the invitation. Perhaps it's time for you to learn to say yes.

The Gift of Salvation

> For by grace you have been saved through faith, and this is not your own doing; it is the gift of God— not the result of works, so that no one may boast. (Eph. 2:8–9)

On Valentine's Day, when he was just two years old, I bought our son, David, a helium-filled, heart-shaped balloon—a small gift of my love. David was at an age where he loved presents, and I thought this would be a fun one.

On our way home after work when I said, "I have a present for you," his eyes lit up. He ran into the house, asking, "Where's my present?" He took the balloon I happily handed him but looked rather unimpressed. "Actually, Mommy," he said, "it's not a present." I didn't realize David knew the word *actually,* and so I said, "What?"

"Actually, it's not a present," he repeated. I had forgotten that to David a present was something in a box with wrapping paper on it. The balloon wasn't in a box. It didn't have any wrapping paper. He was expecting something else, and so actually, it didn't seem like a present.

That incident made me wonder whether there are times when we receive a present from God and don't recognize it. The gift of salvation might be one. Do you know that by welcoming Christ into your life, you have received a gift of unconditional love, forgiveness of sin, and the promise of life eternal? You don't have to unwrap this gift; you just receive it. Actually, it's the greatest gift of all.

Stay Connected to Christ

> Jesus said, "I am the Vine, you are the branches. Those who abide in me and I in them bear much fruit, for apart from me, you can do nothing." (John 15:5)

I've never been much of a gardener. I'm always amazed when the things I plant actually grow. In the summer of 1991, I planted a pretty ground cover by our parsonage garage. I don't recall the name of the plant, but it had variegated leaves, white and green, and the tag said it could be a perennial. *No way,* I thought. *Not with my luck!* You can imagine my delight the next spring when a couple of the plants began to grow again. I thought their leaves were very pretty. So did three-year-old David. And one day, as a surprise, he ripped most of them from the plants and presented me with a bouquet. "Here, Mommy," he said. "I picked this for you." I tried to appear pleased even as I explained that the leaves would quickly die now that they had been disconnected from the plant. Without their source, they were done for, and we watched them quickly wither. Don't let that happen to you. Stay connected to Christ through prayer, worship, and your church family.

Real Nourishment

> Jesus said to them, "I am the bread of life. Whoever comes to me will never be hungry." (John 6:35)

Serving in Knoxville, Iowa, gave Bob and me the new and wonderful experience of being small-town pastors. In such a community, ministers sometimes become widely known. A factor making that so for us was our church's weekly live broadcast of the 8:30 a.m. worship service on a Knoxville radio station. The goal of this radio ministry was to reach homebound members, but anyone could listen to our weekly service.

One week I preached a sermon called "Spiritual Junk Food," suggesting that sometimes we fill our souls with junk, just like we do our bodies. Our family, at the time, was not immune from eating junk food. Our son, David, was in elementary school and often took his lunch to school. In my sermon, I confessed that I tried to pack a nutritious sandwich and raw veggies or fruit for his lunch, but he always wanted a Lunchable.

Lunchables were easy to find on the grocery shelf—a snack pack of processed cheese and meat, ready to eat and tasty but extremely high in salt and having little nutritional value. However, David was persistent, so I had gotten in the habit of buying him one Lunchable a week as a treat, even though I knew it was junk food. "Shame on me," I said in my sermon.

On that very Sunday afternoon, I made a trip to the grocery store. As I passed the snack aisle, I automatically—almost unconsciously—dropped a Lunchable in my grocery cart. Immediately a woman I had never met before appeared beside me, sternly grabbed my arm, and said, "I know who you are, and I saw what you just put in your cart." And then she was gone. That was the last Lunchable I ever bought!

In our day-to-day lives, we don't always have another human being watching over our shoulders when we make junky choices, but God is watching and very likely is whispering in our ears, "I know who you are, and I saw what you just put in your life." Why not try Jesus, the Bread of Life, instead? That's real nourishment!

Follow the Leader

> As Jesus was walking along, he saw a man called Matthew sitting at the tax booth; and he said to him, "Follow me." And he got up and followed him. (Matt. 9:9)

In the spring of 2012, our church in Ankeny was given a wonderful example of following. The enclosed courtyard just outside my office was used primarily as our preschool play area, but that spring, a mother duck decided to make it her nesting ground. The nest was well hidden beneath the bushes, so we didn't realize what was happening until suddenly we had fourteen baby ducklings. I have to admit some of us were getting less work done because we'd become serious duck watchers.

I quickly noticed that the mama duck expected her ducklings to follow, and she became a good springtime Christ symbol for me. She didn't necessarily quack at her ducklings. She just stood tall and gave them a serious look, and generally when she moved, they moved.

Early on, we human beings sometimes frightened the ducklings. If we got too close, they would scatter in all directions, bumping into each other, falling down, and sometimes forgetting to follow their mother. We can be like that. When something disrupts our lives, we get scared or become self-concerned, and we make mistakes. We run in all kinds of crazy directions. We bump into each other. We fall down. That's going to happen. We're going to mess up because we're only human.

But like that mama duck, the risen Christ is not going to yell at us. He won't say, "Stupid, human, why did you do that?" Instead, he will give us that serious look of love, beckon with his eyes, and speak to our hearts, saying, "Follow me."

CHAPTER 4

Forgiven and Forgiving

Forgive

> For if you forgive others their trespasses, your
> heavenly Father will also forgive you; but if you do
> not forgive others, neither will your Father forgive
> your trespasses. (Matt. 6:14–15)

My great-great-grandfather, Joseph Dalton, was convicted
of treason against the United States of America. A Confederate
soldier from West Virginia, he was captured by the Union army
in 1864, charged with treason, and imprisoned at Camp Chase in
Columbia, Ohio. I'm not sure what the penalty might have been
for all those Confederate soldiers like Joseph Dalton. Would it have
been hanging or the firing squad? I don't know what fighting my
great-great grandfather saw in the Civil War, but as the war drew
toward its conclusion, there was still plenty of bitterness and a desire
for revenge on both sides of the Mason-Dixon line.

So I'm grateful that President Abraham Lincoln was talking to
God about what to do with those who fought on the losing side of
the Civil War. He decided not on punishment but on forgiveness
although many were no doubt disappointed with his decision.

Remember the great words from his second inaugural address: "With malice toward none; with charity for all; with firmness in the right, as God gives us to see the right, let us strive on to finish the work we are in; to bind up the nation's wounds; to care for him who shall have borne the battle, and for his widow and his orphan, to do all which may achieve and cherish a just and lasting peace among ourselves and with all nations."[1]

Because of Lincoln's merciful spirit, my great-great-grandfather was allowed to return to West Virginia where he got married and started a family. It's humbling to realize I might not have been born without Lincoln's decision to forgive and to grant amnesty to the Confederate prisoners of war. I wonder what good God might do today if we found the courage to love our enemies.

The Wideness of God's Mercy

> For I will forgive their iniquity, and remember their sin no more. (Jer. 31:34)

God forgives our sin. That's an amazing promise. Knowing that of our free will, we human beings will mess up, sinning against God and others, God promises to forgive our sin.

As my dad faced his final illness, he had one major spiritual problem: he could not believe God had forgiven him. He had regrets. Perhaps he felt he had not been a perfect husband, father, or brother; maybe he sensed he had been an underachiever—not using to the fullest the gifts God had given him. I'm not sure I knew all my father's regrets. But my dad's sense of regret got so severe that one of his Catholic friends persuaded a priest to drop by to see my Methodist dad, in hopes that a more Catholic approach to confession and forgiveness might give him some relief. But even that didn't help, and I think my dad went to his grave without the assurance he was forgiven.

Don't let it be that way for you. No matter what you have done or not done, God always offers a fresh start. Sometimes it's harder to forgive yourself than to forgive others, but know that God forgives you, and in that knowledge, perhaps you can find the ability to forgive yourself. You can't change the past, but God can transform it.

I like the words from an old hymn, "There Is Wideness in God's Mercy."[2] I read this verse at my father's memorial service, more for Dad than for the congregation:

For the love of God is broader than the measure of our mind; and the heart of the Eternal is most wonderfully kind.

I know my dad experienced that broad love of God—the wonderfully kind heart of our Creator—when he reached his heavenly home. I'm just sorry it took him so long to know God's forgiving love. Don't let it be so for you.

It's Not All about You

When God saw what the Ninevites did, how they turned from their evil ways, God changed his mind about the calamity that he had said he would bring upon them; and he did not do it. But this was very displeasing to Jonah, and he became angry. (Jonah 3:10–4:1)

I was not a model child. Like most other kids, I wanted everything done my way—and right now! My grandfather Dalton loved to recount an episode that happened when I was three years old. Gramps, as we called him, had been disabled in an automobile accident and had little use of his legs, although he could get around slowly with crutches. Because of his disability, my grandmother worked full time, but Gramps was available as one of our favorite babysitters.

One day, Gramps was pushing me on our backyard swing.

He couldn't push me very high because he had to use one hand to prop himself up on his crutches. That made me mad. "Put down those crutches and swing me high!" I said. "I can't, honey. I'll fall down," Gramps replied. So I did what any self-respecting three-year-old would do. I hurled myself down on the ground, kicking and screaming, and threw a fit.

I remember that story with some pain, eased only by the fact that my grandfather loved to tease me about it. It's a reminder that as children, we all feel we are at the center of our worlds. Self-centeredness is the realm of small children, but as we mature, we are called to focus not on ourselves but on others. God tried repeatedly to get that message across to Jonah, who threw a fit when God forgave the Ninevites. Sometimes I'm still more like Jonah or that self-centered little girl than I want to admit. How about you?

Confession Is Good for the Soul

> If we say that we have no sin, we deceive ourselves, and the truth is not in us. If we confess our sins, he who is faithful and just will forgive us our sins and cleanse us from all unrighteousness. (1 John 1:8–9)

When I was seven or eight years old, I accidentally broke my mother's glass pitcher, the one she used every evening to make iced tea. I don't remember how I did it, but no one was around to observe my mishap. I was sure Mom would be furious with me, so rather than confessing what I'd done, I hid the pieces of the pitcher amid storage boxes in the basement underneath the stairs. *She'll never look there*, I thought.

That night, as she was getting ready for dinner, Mom asked me, "Have you seen the iced tea pitcher?"

"Me?" I asked. "Why would I? I don't drink iced tea." I lied to my mother, and it felt awful! I started feeling terribly guilty, not just for breaking the pitcher, which was an accident, but for lying about it, which was not.

Several days went by, and every day, Mom would ask, "Martha, are you sure you haven't seen that pitcher?"

"No!" I exclaimed. "I haven't seen the *stupid* pitcher." With each passing day, I felt worse, weighed down by my wrongdoing. Finally, before Mom could ask her nightly question, I broke out in tears and, sobbing, took her by the hand and led her to the broken pitcher (which she had discovered several days earlier).

I told her the whole story and waited for the punishment I knew I deserved. But my mother took her sobbing child in her arms, held me for the longest time, and said over and over, "I forgive you, honey. I love you." I don't remember if there was some punishment for my misdeed. What I do remember is the huge relief I felt at being forgiven—and still being loved by my mom—despite what I had done wrong. This same kind of forgiving love is offered to each of us whenever we confess our sin to God, who loves us unconditionally.

Lessons from Temptation

> And lead us not into temptation, but deliver us from evil. (Matt. 6:13 KJV)

In eighth-grade home economics class, I once cheated on a test. This happened in cooking class, and I remember it well. We were seated at square tables in individual kitchen areas, and all four of us at my table decided to pass around our completed test papers to compare answers while the teacher wasn't looking. But she did look and saw me passing my paper.

None of the other girls was caught, and while I did not fail the test, on my next report card there was a large red N (which meant "Not Satisfactory") in the conduct category of "Self-Control." When my father looked over the report card and saw that N, you would have thought it was the worst mark anyone had ever received. In my defense, I said it had been unfairly given only to me since everyone at my table had misbehaved. That caused Dad to storm the school, find the teacher, and demand to know how such a thing could happen to his perfect daughter. And she told him I had cheated on a test. Well, my father stormed home and in no uncertain terms told me that N was indeed the worst mark I could receive. I had given in to the temptation to cheat and had learned the hard way that it was a bad idea. You can be sure I never gave in to that temptation again! Look back on your own moral failures, and let them be your teachers.

Just Plain Old Sin

> I do not understand my own actions. For I do not
> do what I want, but I do the very thing I hate. Now
> if I do what I do not want, I agree that the law is
> good. But in fact it is no longer I that do it, but sin
> that dwells within me. (Rom. 7:15–17)

Before leaving for a 1964 high school trip to Germany, I stopped over to say good-bye to my Dalton grandparents, and Gramps handed me five dollars. With a twinkle in his eye he said, "Do something you're not supposed to do with this money." I put the money carefully in my pocket, and I confess I did not forget his instruction. Normally a teenager who did not break the rules, I suddenly felt like I had been given special permission. The 1964 edition of *Europe on 5 Dollars a Day* reminded me you could do a lot with just five dollars!

Finally, my big chance came. Before departing, our leader said we would have an opportunity to ride on a glider with a trained pilot, but we needed our parents' signed permission. My parents thought it was scary enough just to let me go to Europe! The thought of me gliding around in the air was too much, and they hadn't signed the permission slip. But the glider ride cost only five dollars. So, when the day arrived, I pulled my grandfather's five dollars from my pocket, forged my parents' signatures on a permission slip, and up I went. I knew what I was doing was wrong, and yet I did it.

Shortly after the pilot and I were up in the small glider, a rainstorm began. The glider, which had been flying so smoothly, started bumping up and down. I was terrified and felt grateful when the pilot muttered German words I could understand: "We have to land." We landed safely, thank goodness, but at the far end of the field, and I had to help the pilot push the glider all the way back in the pouring rain. I've always wondered if that sudden rainstorm was just a coincidence.

But why did I do that? I knew better. I realized it wasn't right to forge my parents' signatures, but doing the wrong thing looked exciting. There's a three-letter word for that phenomenon: sin. We commit sin anytime we separate ourselves from God's intentions for us in thought, word, or deed—anytime we give in to that evil nature instead of doing the good God desires. In Romans 7, the apostle Paul addresses this human capacity to choose sin. Thank goodness for the grace of God, who through Jesus Christ forgives our foolishness and sin.

Taming the Tongue

> For every species of beast and bird, of reptile and sea
> creature, can be tamed and has been tamed by the
> human species, but no one can tame the tongue—a
> restless evil, full of deadly poison. (James 3:7–8)

As a teenager, I regarded myself as a leader in my small circle of friends. For a time in junior high, the group took up my maiden name Dalton, and we called ourselves the Dalton Gang. Compared with gangs today, we were fairly harmless. We didn't have any weapons; we didn't use drugs. We didn't beat up other people—not physically. But maybe we did verbally. I, for one, made it very clear when I didn't like someone, and I expected others to agree with me or at least to think I was very clever.

I remember vividly a comment I made one evening as our group was driving to a high school basketball game. I was elaborating long and loud on how "sickeningly sweet" I thought another girl in our class was. I will never forget how one member of our group said very quietly, "Please stop the car. The girl you are making fun of is my friend, and if you continue to talk that way about her, I will get out and walk to the game."

I can't describe exactly how I felt at that moment. It was as though truth had slapped me in the face. I had been confronted about my sin. I now knew who was sickening, and it was not the person I had been belittling!

I mumbled "I'm sorry" and wished the car would stop not so my friend could get out but so I might run from that place, bury myself in a hole, and never be seen again. It is painful to be confronted about one's sin! That night I began changing the way I spoke of others and also the way I thought of them.

As an adult, I often returned to my hometown for a few days at Christmas. While there, I would see high school friends, including the friend who had confronted me so long ago. She perhaps forgot the incident and would update me on the lives of our mutual acquaintances, including the person I had once belittled. I would remember my youthful arrogance with pain and utter again a prayer that has been a theme of my life: "O God, help me to be kind—in my words and my speech, kind to everyone."

From Guilt to Grace

> If we confess our sins, God who is faithful and
> just will forgive us our sins and cleanse us from all
> unrighteousness. (1 John 1:9)

I remember with regret a time during college when I let down a friend. I had offered to help my roommate with a big sorority event she was running. It was scheduled for a Saturday afternoon in the spring. At the time, I wasn't dating anyone. My social life was, in my own estimation, pretty pitiful. So when I got a call from a guy inviting me to go sailing on a nearby lake on Saturday afternoon, I instantly said, "Sure, I'd love to."

I'd like to say I forgot I already had committed my Saturday afternoon, but in actuality I decided a date was more important. I didn't tell my friend in advance. I just failed to show up when it came time to help with her event. Somebody else had to tell her, "I saw Martha leave earlier with some guy."

It was a beautiful Saturday afternoon, and I wish I could say I had a great time sailing, but mostly I remember having this awful feeling that I had messed up. I felt guilty. And when I got back, my roommate was there, looking angry and disappointed. "Where on earth were you?" she asked. "Why did you do that to me? You really let me down." I didn't deserve to be forgiven, but I confessed, and because she was a person of grace she forgave me and we're still friends today. I never made that mistake again, but there have been lots of other times when I've been grateful for the forgiving love of God and of other people.

Driving Out Unclean Spirits

> Just then there was in their synagogue a man with
> an unclean spirit, and he cried out, "What have you

to do with us, Jesus of Nazareth? Have you come to destroy us? I know who you are, the Holy One of God." But Jesus rebuked him, saying, "Be silent, and come out of him!" And the unclean spirit, convulsing him and crying with a loud voice, came out of him. (Mark 1:23–26)

In Jesus's day, people who were mentally ill or who had seizure-causing illnesses like epilepsy were said to be possessed by unclean spirits or demons. We might not call it that today, but most of us have had experience with this reality. I've known demons in my own history.

We could start with demon rum. It killed my uncle, my father's only brother. My uncle was a great guy—a World War II veteran, a car salesman who helped me buy my first car—but he was addicted to alcohol. On his own, he seemed powerless to free himself from this unclean spirit; he seemed possessed. His demon ultimately led him through two failed marriages, cost him his job, and left him in a dingy basement apartment, where he died alone of cirrhosis of the liver.

My mother was also a victim of an unclean spirit. The Scripture says, "Honor your father and your mother" (Ex. 20:12). I want to do that because I was blessed with two terrific parents who loved me and my two brothers more than they loved life itself. But my mom was not herself in her later years. She was bothered by headaches, but those weren't her demons. The demons came with the prescription painkillers, which were addictive for my mother. When those medications were combined with her cigarette and alcohol use, my mom seemed to be possessed. I've known some unclean spirits. You probably have too.

Early in our ministry Bob and I tried to face off the demon of domestic violence. A couple attended worship almost every Sunday and seemed to have a happy young family. Then the wife shared with us that her husband, who struggled with alcohol, was regularly beating her. She called for help late one night, and together we went to their home. We did our best to take the power of Jesus with us, but as the husband pinned Bob against the garage wall in anger, I wished we had invited law enforcement to come along.

What does it look like when God sets someone free today? It could be as dramatic as the story in the Scripture passage above, but I believe the liberating, healing work of Christ in our times is often quite subtle. If you aren't looking carefully, you may miss it. Today it is likelier to be that glimmer of hope in the eye of someone who for the first time reaches out to an individual or a group and gets the support needed to step away from the bondage of addiction. Or perhaps it comes in the form of a hug when you've just shared your spiritual struggle and others have prayed for you, reminding you that you're not alone. Or it could be the peace that comes in the silence of prayer when you sense that your inner burden is lighter—that you have indeed been forgiven, healed, and set free by the love of Christ. May you know that power, which is greater than any demon you may face.

Judgment or Responsibility?

> For all of us must appear before the judgment seat of Christ, so that each may receive recompense for what has been done in the body, whether good or evil. (2 Cor. 5:10)

Sometime in the 1980s (before cell phones), Bob and I were backpacking in the Colorado Rockies. We camped in the wilderness away from any means of communication for several days, so when we returned to civilization, I used a pay phone to let my parents know we were safe. The first thing my mother said upon hearing my voice was, "The bishop wants to talk to you." We United Methodist clergy are appointed by the bishop, and when the bishop calls, you pay attention!

Now the bishop and my mother were not in the habit of carrying on regular conversations. In fact, my mother, who lived in Kansas, had never met the Iowa bishop. To get my parents' phone number, the bishop's secretary had to do some digging in my professional file. As luck would have it, I called my parents on a Friday evening, and the bishop would not be back in his office until the following Monday morning. So over the weekend I was left to wonder, *What does the bishop want?* I was pretty sure he didn't call to tell us we were being considered for a move, because it was the wrong time of year for that, and after all, he didn't call for Bob and me—just for me. "The bishop wants to talk to *you*," my mother said. What could be so important that the bishop would try to track me down on vacation?

I finally decided I must have done something wrong, but what? Sometimes we clergy make people mad, and I could think of a few folks who might be angry with me. Maybe I hadn't been making enough pastoral calls; maybe it was my sermons; maybe I'd inadvertently done something terrible. Perhaps that phone call would be like going before a judge, but I had no idea of the possible charges against me. I think that's how many of us may feel about judgment day. We have read in Scripture that there will be some kind of final accounting, but we aren't sure exactly when or how we have fallen short.

After my relaxing vacation was interrupted by a weekend of extreme anxiety, I phoned the bishop's office on Monday morning to learn he just wanted to ask me to serve on a committee. There was a deadline for getting the names of committee members printed in the conference journal. That's why his secretary tracked me down—for a printing deadline!

When I returned that phone call, I thought I would experience judgment, but it turned out I got a new responsibility. Maybe that's how it will be for us when we reach heaven's gates—not just a time of judgment but a time when we get our heavenly assignment and continue in service to our risen Lord.

Atonement for Sin Is Not a Self-improvement Project

> But as it is, Christ has appeared once for all at the end of the age to remove sin by the sacrifice of himself. (Heb. 9:28)

Someone once said, "Every home improvement project requires at least three trips to Home Depot." If you've ever tackled one of those projects, I suspect you know the truth of this comment. A project never turns out to be quite as simple or inexpensive as it appeared on the surface, and sometimes you make matters worse instead of better.

Bob and I lived in church-owned parsonages for more than thirty years. While we had church trustees available to handle parsonage maintenance, that didn't keep us from trying one do-it-yourself project at our parsonage in Waterloo. It was an older two-story home with a large attic reached by stairs from a second-floor bedroom.

There was no attic insulation, so we were losing a lot of heat through the roof, leading to high utility bills. We decided to blow cellulose insulation into the attic, which seemed like something we could do ourselves—no need to bother the trustees. We understood the process. One person feeds insulation into a blower machine on the ground; the insulation goes through a long hose up to the attic, and another person standing in the attic directs the hose, blowing insulation to the proper places. What could be hard about that?

Picture this scene. It's a sunny summer day. I'm stationed in the backyard with the machine and a small mountain of bags of insulation, and Bob is up in the attic with the hose. It's a pretty big attic with one small window, and the temperature up there is about

110 degrees. Bob is wearing protective clothing—long-sleeve shirt, gloves, and mask.

We start off pretty well, but it takes me a while to get the rhythm of loading the blower. The insulation bags are heavy when full and messy to pour into the machine, and if I go too fast, the hose jams. Then poor Bob in the hot attic has to wait until I clean out the hose and start again, and sometimes I hear words from the attic usually reserved for the golf course!

I don't remember how many hours this project took us, but it was a long and miserable time! Bob was sweltering, banging his head on the attic beams, and hurriedly shoving the hose into all the nooks and crannies of the attic. Finally, I yelled up to Bob, "How much more insulation can that attic possibly hold? Aren't we done yet?" Eventually, he hollered out the window, "You can stop."

I waited for him to come downstairs ... and waited ... and waited until I heard a few more golf course words. Then Bob's face appeared at the attic window, and he told me he had filled up not only the attic floor but had unknowingly shoved the hose through the drywall and had filled up the attic stairwell. He was trapped in the attic. To get out, he had to lower a rope onto which I tied a snow shovel. Bob hauled that up through the window and dug himself out of the attic. There are some things you shouldn't try to do yourself!

That's true far beyond the realm of home improvement. Consider the reclamation of our souls. The epistle to the Hebrews reminds us that atoning for our sins is one of those things we're foolish to try to do ourselves. Because we are mortal, flawed human beings, we will mess up—sometimes royally.

All of us sin and fall short of the glory of God. All of us get ourselves into messes we can't shovel out of all by ourselves. But here's the good news. God's grace is offered to us today and every day. As the writer of Hebrews says, "once and for all" through his death on the cross, Christ has atoned for our sins—and the sins of the whole world—and now intercedes for us at the right hand of

God. We probably could have learned how to properly insulate our attic by ourselves, but only Christ can rescue us from sin.

God's Forgiveness

> God does not deal with us according to our sins, nor repay us according to our iniquities. For as the heavens are high above the earth, so great is God's steadfast love toward those who fear him. (Ps. 103:10–11)

One Sunday after church, our seven-year-old son, David, announced, "I know something God can't do." Curious, we asked, "What's that?" He replied, "God can't not forgive." Despite the grammatical double negative, David touched on an important truth. God freely forgives us— again and again and again—with no strings attached. God forgives because God loves us so much and wants to be in relationship with us.

God could choose not to forgive. "Vengeance is mine," says the Lord (Deut. 32:35). God has the power to seek revenge for all our evil deeds, but that is not God's way. God wills forgiveness; God wants to forgive. It is in the nature of God to forgive us.

CHAPTER 5

Timeless Truths from Jesus

Older Brother Complex

> He replied, "Your brother has come, and your father
> has killed the fatted calf, because he has got him
> back safe and sound." Then he became angry and
> refused to go in. His father came out and began to
> plead with him. (Luke 15:27–28)

The two brothers in Jesus's great parable of the prodigal son
remind me of my father and his younger brother. They both served
in World War II, my dad in the navy and my uncle in the army.
My uncle was a prodigal son. When he returned from the war, he
married and had a couple of kids. Then he started drinking heavily,
and the marriage broke up. He kept on drinking, but he had a great
personality and soon married again, had three more children, and
after several years divorced again. He was a used car salesman, but
because of his heavy drinking, his business went up and down, and
he was frequently out of money, often coming to family to bail
him out.

My dad, on the other hand, was similar to the older brother in
Jesus's parable. Although he was by no means perfect, he was the

dutiful son who faithfully supported his wife and kids and looked out for his aging parents. Initially he tried to help my uncle out of financial jams, but he soon came to see his brother as a drunken con man and refused to help. Their relationship was severed, and Dad was furious to learn my uncle had gone to my aging grandmother for money.

When Grandma's physical and mental health deteriorated, Dad finally had to place her in a nursing home. She was there quite some time, but her younger son never came to see her. That made my father livid, and so when Grandma died, my dad decided not to tell my uncle. "Let him read about it in the paper," he said. Fortunately, my mother persuaded him otherwise, and my father and my uncle were together at my grandmother's funeral. They even shook hands when the service was over, and I hoped maybe that was the beginning of a reconciliation. Regrettably, it turned out to be the last time they saw each other. A few years later, in the small basement apartment where he lived alone, my uncle died of cirrhosis of the liver.

There's a deep sadness about their story because my uncle, unlike the Prodigal Son, never came to his senses, to the best of my knowledge. The Prodigal Son had one of those moments of realization—as if a light bulb went on in his head—and he thought, *How could I have made such a mistake? How could I have been so ungrateful? I don't just need food. I need my father. I need to go home.* My uncle never got to that point. Maybe the disease of alcoholism kept him from it. I don't know for sure. I think my father, many years later as he approached his own death, carried regret that he and his brother could never reconcile.

My uncle and my dad never experienced reunion in their earthly lives. But I am not without hope for them because as Christians we know this life is not the end of the story. I trust that in their heavenly home, God is still working on those two headstrong men, reconciling them to each other and drawing them very close to God's heart.

Ready or Not

> Therefore you also must be ready, for the Son of
> Man is coming at an unexpected hour. (Matt.
> 24:44)

Summer evenings meant hide-and-seek in my childhood
neighborhood. As the sun was setting, all the children on our block
would gather to see if we could hide so well that the one who was
"it" could not find us. I remember my favorite hiding places: the
out-of-the-way corner of the neighbor's porch across the street or
the narrow space between the bushes and the ground in front of our
house. I would run to these or other places as the one designated "it"
patiently counted one ... two ... three.

Then came the alert: "Here I come, ready or not." Inevitably,
one of two things would happen to me in those next few minutes.
Sometimes, in my haste to hide, I would forget to make sure I was
totally concealed. A shirt sleeve or pant leg sticking out around the
corner would betray me, and I would be caught. Or sometimes the
one who was "it" took so long in searching for me that I would begin
to daydream until suddenly I was startled back to reality with the
words "I found you!"

"Here I come, ready or not." The kingdom of God can break in
at any time. Jesus told us to be alert, be watchful, and be ready, for
we do not know the day or the hour. We could apply these words
exclusively to thinking about the end time, or the second coming
of Christ. But I suggest we apply these words to ourselves right now
by acknowledging that today is the day. Every day is the day, and
every hour is the hour. In this and every moment, we are called to
be accountable. Are we ready for God's kingdom to break in on our
lives?

As a young girl, I used to get caught in hide-and-seek because I
was careless in my preparation or had become apathetic about it. If
we as Christ's people are going to be prepared, we must be sensitive

to the needs of the world and must respond to those needs as best we can. We need to be ready for God's kingdom to break in, and we do that by doing our best to act as God's people on this day, in this hour.

How Not to Make Disciples

> Go therefore and make disciples of all nations. (Matt. 28:19)

Sometimes we have a negative response to the word *evangelism*. For me that perspective comes from an experience I had as a freshman in college. The scene was the busy student union lunch spot. All of a sudden, in the midst of the crowd, I was approached by a young woman from one of my classes. She grabbed me by the elbow with a look of urgency in her eyes and asked, "Martha, have you been saved?"

I had been baptized and raised in the church, gone to Sunday school, been confirmed, and occasionally attended a youth group. I was even going to church while I was away at college. But her question caught me off guard and I hesitated, saying, "Uh, well ..." In an instant she had whisked me to a nearby table, and before I had a chance to say anything, she laid out a diagram about the cross, quoted Scripture, and said, "Let's pray right now for your salvation."

But as she bowed her head in prayer, I saw my chance to escape, quickly said, "Sorry, I'm late for class," and hurried away as fast as I could. No doubt her intentions were good, but the effect of her actions on me was not! I prefer the approach commonly attributed to St. Francis of Assisi: "Preach the gospel at all times. If necessary, use words."

People, Get Ready

> Heaven and earth will pass away, but my words will
> not pass away. But about that day and hour no one
> knows, neither the angels of heaven, nor the Son,
> but only the Father. (Matt. 24:35–36)

In the mid-seventies, while living in Cedar Rapids, Iowa, Bob and I arranged to take the train to Colorado to go skiing with friends. The closest Amtrak stop to Cedar Rapids was the Iowa town of Mount Pleasant. When we got there, the station attendant said, "The train is running about an hour late." Thinking we had time to grab a bite to eat, we found a restaurant in Mount Pleasant, had a nice dinner, and returned to the station just in time to see our train pulling away from the station without us. We ran inside the station to ask the attendant to stop the train, but she said, "Sorry, I can't do that." As we watched our skiing vacation go down the drain, she said, "I can call to ask them to try to hold the train for you at the next stop in Ottumwa, but you'll have to hurry." So off we went.

Between Mount Pleasant and Ottumwa, the train track happens to parallel the highway. Most of the time, as we sped along, we could see our train! Sometimes we were a little ahead of it, but most of the time it was in front of us and getting further ahead by the minute. Our drive reminded me of a chase scene in an old Keystone Cops movie. The tricky times were driving through the small towns along the way, with their lower speed limits and stop signs. Bob would say something like, "You watch for the cops," and we'd zoom through.

There was one other challenge on our journey. In the mid-seventies, our country was in an oil crisis, and most service stations were closed on Sunday to save gas. We were almost out of gas and planning to return on a Sunday, so we had to stop at a filling station when we got to Ottumwa. All this was happening before cell phones, so while Bob filled the gas tank, I used a pay phone to notify the depot we were on our way. The attendant said, "You'd better hurry!"

When we got to the station, which we had a little difficulty finding (no GPS back then either), we pulled our bags from the car and ran to the train, which fortunately was still there. The conductor looked at us and then at our car and said, "You might want to close your trunk."

Once on board, we learned that our sleeper car had been sold between Mount Pleasant and Ottumwa, so we had to sit in the coach car all night. However, we were so thankful to be on the train, we didn't care except that all around us other passengers were muttering about the additional delay on account of some dummies who missed the train back in Mount Pleasant.

In 1965, at least a decade before Bob and I missed that train, singer and songwriter Curtis Mayfield wrote a song about being alert to Christ's coming. He was a member of the Impressions, an African American rhythm and blues group, and wrote the song after being inspired by the 1964 civil rights march on Washington.

> People get ready
> There's a train a-coming.
> You don't need no baggage.
> You just get on board.
> All you need is faith
> To hear the diesels humming.
> You don't need no ticket.
> You just thank the Lord.[1]

Bob and I were grateful to catch the train to Colorado that we almost missed. But we just thank the Lord that through faith, we need not worry about missing the ride of our lives with Christ.

Loving the "Least of These" Isn't Easy

> Then they also will answer, "Lord, when was it that
> we saw you hungry or thirsty or a stranger or naked
> or sick or in prison, and did not take care of you?"
> Then he will answer them, "Truly I tell you, just as
> you did not do it to one of the least of these, you did
> not do it to me." (Matt. 25:44–45)

Have you ever looked in the face of Jesus? I believe I have at least once, and I ended up calling the cops. Or maybe Bob called the police, or perhaps it was one of the other students who lived in our seminary housing in Berkeley, California. The event took place so long ago that I'm not sure.

Jesus came to us in the form of a mentally ill homeless man who took up residence in the carport at our seminary apartment complex. In the San Francisco Bay area, the climate is so temperate that it is possible to live outside all year round. In the late 1970s many homeless people did that. They made their homes in bushes and doorways, and this fellow chose our carport—or rather a storage area just outside the carport.

He probably was one of the mentally ill persons no longer housed in state institutions, with few places to go except the streets. He wasn't very old, but he made unusual sounds instead of speaking, and we found him scary looking. Those of us in the apartment complex told him he couldn't live in our storeroom, and we locked that door. He then moved into our laundry room, but his personal hygiene left quite a bit to be desired, so we locked that door.

When it got a bit cooler outside, he moved into our building's furnace room. One night when Bob went to check the heat, he tripped over this man in the dark, scaring them both to death! So we locked that door, and the man moved up on the building's flat roof, which doubled as a sun deck in warm weather. He simply would not leave our building, and finally we called the police, who took him away. He never bothered us again.

I always felt bad about how we handled that situation. Here I was training to be a minister, yet I was so afraid of the fellow that I don't think I ever asked him his name. I don't believe I was ever kind to him. I certainly didn't try to figure out how he happened to be homeless or what I could do about it. In terms of Jesus's parable in Matthew 25, in which he speaks of separating the sheep from the goats, I was a goat. When we see Jesus face to face in the "least of these," sometimes we don't know what to do, so we do nothing. In cases like this fellow, any human judge would certainly say we had done the wise and prudent thing, but what about the divine judge? What would Jesus say?

The Cruciform Life

> He called the crowd with his disciples, and said to them, "If any want to become my followers, let them deny themselves and take up their cross and follow me. For those who want to save their life will lose it, and those who lose their life for my sake, and for the sake of the gospel, will save it." (Mark 8:34–35)

The Rev. Don Maple was the pastor at Lovely Lane United Methodist Church in Cedar Rapids, Iowa, in the 1970s. As a young married couple, Bob and I were members there. Lovely Lane was the church that sent us off into ministry, and when we were done with seminary, Don Maple was moving to a new pastoral appointment at Grace United Methodist Church in Waterloo, and we had been appointed as his associates. So, both as church members and as new clergy, we had a chance to benefit from Don's expertise and mentoring.

Bob and I didn't always agree with everything Don said in his sermons. We thought his recurring message was "To be a Christian means to take up your cross every day and to follow Jesus," and there were weeks when we wanted to hear something less challenging. In fact, one Easter Sunday, we had found his sermon so maddening that on the drive home from church, Bob and I rolled up our car windows so no one would hear us and screamed at the top of our lungs.

Nonetheless, we learned many things from Don, one of the most important being that Christians are supposed to live a cruciform lifestyle. *Cruciform* is a term that comes from traditional church architecture. Medieval churches were often built in cruciform—in the form of a cross. Don always said that is how we Christians are supposed to live our lives. He stressed that this means living sacrificially as servants, giving ourselves so others can know life.

In a world where everything is so self-centered, God calls Christians to a different way. That's what led us into the ministry—a desire for God to use our lives for some greater good. Don Maple died in May 2013, and we are grateful for all he taught us as our pastor, mentor, and friend.

Blessed Are the Poor

> Then he looked up at his disciples and said: "Blessed are you who are poor, for yours is the kingdom of God." (Luke 6:20)

Ray was an older man in our Waterloo Grace congregation. He was World War II veteran who had lost an arm in the war. On Sundays, he always wore the same old black suit coat with one sleeve pinned up. As far as we knew, Ray had no immediate family; a disability pension was his only income; his home was a room in an old downtown hotel.

Some church members didn't like being around Ray. He looked

unkempt and talked in grunts. He sat at the back of the sanctuary for worship, but we knew he was there, because if the service went longer than an hour, Ray would get restless and grunt loudly from his pew. We never needed a clock because we had Ray.

Ray would also show up whenever there was food at the church. It didn't matter if it was a potluck or a Bible study; it didn't matter if he was in the group or not. Ray was there to eat—not to talk, just to eat. That might have been okay with the good people of the church if it hadn't been for his smell. Ray had a terrible body odor. Perhaps he couldn't bathe adequately with his physical disability; maybe he didn't have bathing facilities at the hotel; maybe he had no way to wash his clothes; maybe he didn't have any other clothes. Anyway, the problem generated much discussion and finally some action.

It was decided that the friendliest woman in the congregation, who was always kind to Ray, needed to talk with him about how he smelled. Bless her heart, she said she'd do it. She had quite a long talk with Ray, but it didn't change anything except that he stopped coming to some of the free eating opportunities at the church. It's possible that her conversation with Ray was the longest one anyone in the church ever had with him. Wouldn't it be terrible if the longest conversation anyone ever had with you was about your body odor? You might ask yourself, *Does anybody really care?*

Sometime after we moved from Waterloo to our next appointment, the pastor who took our place phoned to say Ray had died. That led me to remember a few other things about Ray. We had once studied attendance patterns at the church. Many members were in worship most Sundays, but few were always there. Ray was always there; he never missed a Sunday until he became ill. We also studied giving patterns and learned that Ray was one of our most faithful givers. He didn't give huge amounts, for he had a very small income. But we could tell by the size and regularity of his gifts that Ray was a tither; he gave 10 percent of his meager income to God through the church.

To some people, Ray looked, acted, and smelled like the kind of poor person who makes us uncomfortable. But to God, he looked, acted, and probably even smelled like a beloved child. May we look at the people and the needs of our world with God's eyes.

WWJD?

> And as he sat at dinner in Levi's house, many tax collectors and sinners were also sitting with Jesus and his disciples—for there were many who followed him. When the scribes of the Pharisees saw that he was eating with sinners and tax collectors, they said to his disciples, "Why does he eat with tax collectors and sinners?" When Jesus heard this, he said to them, "Those who are well have no need of a physician, but those who are sick; I have come to call not the righteous but sinners." (Mark 2:15–17)

One Sunday a new young woman came to our church in Knoxville, Iowa. I don't know how she happened to come to us, but church was totally new to her. She knew very little about Jesus and almost nothing about the Bible, but she came with her four rambunctious children, ages two through ten, in tow. You could tell the children had never been in church, because they ran all over the building and shouted to each other just to hear the echoes in the long halls. During worship they slid up and down the pew, and each needed to go to the bathroom at least once during the service.

This mom enrolled her children in Sunday school and in the Wednesday children's program, and pretty soon she signed up for the new member class. Having no background in the church, she absorbed the information like a sponge, with wide eyes and excited questions. A whole new world was opening up to her. On the day she was received into membership, she was also baptized. You could tell from the smile on her face that it was a moment of great importance to her. She immediately volunteered to help out, especially with children's programming, and was recruited to assist the lead teacher in third-grade Sunday school.

Everything seemed to be going fine until I got a call from our Christian education coordinator late one night. "Did you see the ten o'clock news?" she asked. It seems this young mom and her husband had been arrested for growing and selling marijuana. They were in the country jail, but the mom would be released on bond in the morning. The children had been placed in foster care. Our education coordinator was concerned for this family, but she also asked the practical questions: "What about the Sunday school teaching? What does our child safety program say about this? We can't have people saying, 'Well, son, I guess your Sunday school teacher's a jail bird' or 'Did you know your Sunday school teacher sells drugs?' What shall we do?"

I uttered that sentence ministers say a lot: "I'll pray about it and get back to you tomorrow." Tomorrow came, but before I had a chance to call our educator back, the young mom, now out of jail on bond, called me. As she told her story, she said, "I've really made a bad mistake, but now I need to make it right. I need to get my family back together." Then she added, "You probably don't want me to teach Sunday school anymore, do you?"

I responded, "While you're in this crisis time, it might be confusing for the kids, but more importantly, I think you need some adult support right now. Why not come to the adult class I'm teaching on prayer?"

And she did. What courage it must have taken for her, a newcomer, to walk into a group of church members she didn't know but who may have known her from TV or the newspaper! Maybe because she was such a new Christian, she had not yet been tainted by thoughts that church people might be judgmental or self-righteous. She thought of us as kind and loving, and I prayed we would not disappoint her.

At the end of class, I asked for prayer concerns. I was surprised when this young mom spoke up and had no idea what she would say. She told the whole story to the class, saying, "I came to the church originally because I wanted to better myself and my family, and now I have really messed things up. But I want to make things right, and more than anything, I want my family back together." And the people in the class, bless them, enfolded her in love and caring. We prayed for her, her children, and her husband in jail.

Later when she was visiting her husband, he asked her, "What were you doing about ten-thirty this morning?" She told him about the prayer class, adding, "At ten-thirty, we were praying for you," and he said, "At that time, I felt the most powerful sense of love I have ever felt." The next day, when Bob visited him in jail, her husband—who was not a new Christian but one who had fallen away—recommitted himself to Christ.

Many good things happened for this young woman in the following weeks. Church members reached out to her; they phoned her and sent cards that said, "We're praying for you." You could see her becoming stronger every week. Then one day her husband, now out of jail, came with her to Sunday school. The following week her family was reunited and sitting together in worship. Before long she came to our adult class and said, "I just wanted to say thanks to the class, but I've been asked to please come back to the third-grade Sunday school. They need me there." Amazing things can happen when the church treats people like Jesus did!

The Power of Random Acts of Kindness

> Whoever welcomes a prophet in the name of a prophet will receive a prophet's reward; and whoever welcomes a righteous person in the name of a righteous person will receive the reward of the righteous; and whoever gives even a cup of cold water to one of these little ones in the name of a

disciple—truly I tell you, none of these will lose
their reward. (Matt. 10:41–42)

One day in 1997, out of the blue Bob and I received a letter from
a man who had briefly attended our former church sometime during
the 1980s. It was a reminder to me that sometimes God is using us
even when we don't know it.

The man wrote, "Martha and Bob, I thought that you would
be interested in how a man that you brought back into the fold is
doing after all these years. You more than likely will not remember
me, but you made a massive difference in my life. As a man fresh
out of prison and in the work release program, you showed me just
what spirituality was really all about. The way you both treated me
gave me an entirely new outlook on life. The forgiveness that you
showed me helped me forgive myself for all of the things that I had
done in the past."

As I dusted off my memories of this man, I realized that outside
of time spent in worship, we had probably spent no more than an
hour or two in conversation with him, and yet, without our knowing
or understanding it, God had used us as forces for good in his life.
What a privilege!

No Good Samaritan

Jesus replied, "A man was going down from
Jerusalem to Jericho, and fell into the hands of
robbers, who stripped him, beat him, and went
away, leaving him half dead. Now by chance a
priest was going down that road; and when he saw
him, he passed by on the other side. So likewise a
Levite, when he came to the place and saw him,
passed by on the other side. But a Samaritan while

traveling came near him; and when he saw him, he was moved with pity." (Luke 10:30–33)

One day in 2006 while making regular weekly hospital calls, I was stopped at a red light at a downtown Des Moines intersection. Mine was the only car on the street, and I noticed a man heading in my direction. He was an older down-and-out man with a limp that made it hard for him to move, and yet he came quickly. There was no mistake; he was coming toward me. I locked my door and cautiously rolled the window down a crack as he approached. (The words of my mother rang in my head: "Never talk to strangers.") "Do you have any money for bus fare?" he asked. (The words of homeless shelter experts now crossed my mind: "Never give out cash in these situations.")

Without thinking further, I said, "No, I'm sorry I don't." (Was that a lie or an excuse, or did my words simply mean "Yes, I do have money, but I don't believe I should give it to you"?) As the light turned green and I put my foot on the gas, the man smiled in a sad way and said, "That's okay. God bless you." Feeling like the priest or the Levite in the Good Samaritan story, I drove away.

I had encountered a person in need but did not help him. Perhaps I was right in not giving cash, but maybe I could have done something. I could have asked, "Where are you trying to go?" or "How much do you need?" All the way to the next hospital, I was kicking myself inside. Why did he have to say, "God bless you"? How could God bless me when I had just turned away my neighbor?

The incident haunted me for some time. Every time I drove by that intersection (at least once a week), I found myself looking for that old man and wondering what to do if I saw him. I felt like I might stop the car and run to him saying, "Here, take my money. Just take all of it!" I wonder if the priest and the Levite were haunted after they passed by the poor man lying wounded beside the road without helping him. It's hard to be the Good Samaritan!

A Gift from Prison

> "And when was it that we saw you sick or in prison
> and visited you?" And the king will answer them,
> "Truly I tell you, just as you did it to one of the least
> of these who are members of my family, you did it
> to me." (Matt. 25:39–40)

On Valentine's Day 2008, eight people from our Ankeny
church went to prison. We worshipped at the Women's Correctional
Institution in Mitchellville, Iowa, with the Women at the Well.
That's a United Methodist congregation inside prison walls where
the church members are all inmates. This was the first time our
church attended, but it would not be the last. They welcomed us
warmly as guests, and it was a touching service in many ways. In the
moving prayer time, participants submitted written prayer requests
or spoke their requests aloud. These prayer requests were not for the
faint-hearted; they were prayers for overcoming their failings, prayers
for restoring their marriages, prayers for their children.

At the end of the service, the pastor said, "Before we close, we
have a person who wants to say something." One of the inmates
came to the front of the worship space and spoke.

> I want to say something to the guests here from the
> Ankeny church tonight. I am from Ankeny and
> my son is a student at the middle school near your
> church. It's really hard being here and not being able
> to be with my son. Middle school years are tough. I
> worry about him a lot—but not after school. Every
> day after school he goes to your Jesus Christ Café.
> I talk to him almost every night on the phone, and
> he says he has been to your Jesus Christ Café. And
> I feel good because I know he's safe. I thank God
> and I thank you for Jesus Christ Café.

I wouldn't have traded that moment for a million dollars! Jesus Christ Café (JC's as we called it) was our church's youth center, a small coffee house located behind our uptown building. It was open every day after school, and middle school students dropped in for refreshments, video games, and conversation. Besides young people from our church, we would get a number of students who had no connection with us—perhaps no connection with any church. Some of them had major real-life needs (like the boy whose mother was in prison), and our co-directors of youth ministry did an excellent job of reaching out to them. My experience with the Women at the Well reminded me that sometimes we touch lives in ways we don't even realize. "Lord, when was it that we visited you in prison?"

God's Kingdom in a Borehole

> He put before them another parable: "The kingdom of heaven is like a mustard seed that someone took and sowed in his field; it is the smallest of all the seeds, but when it has grown it is the greatest of shrubs and becomes a tree, so that the birds of the air come and make nests in its branches." (Matt. 13:31–32)

In July 2010, Bob, David, and I, along with nine other members of our Ankeny congregation, traveled to the African nation of Malawi, one of the poorest countries in the world. While the 2010 average per capita annual income in the United States was around $46,000, the average annual income in Malawi was $900—less than three dollars a day.

Our congregation began a relationship with the United Methodist Church of Malawi in 2007. From the outset, our mission to Malawi was one of encouragement—to support the amazing growth of the United Methodist Church there. Our church had donated funds for several boreholes (deep wells) to be drilled, because a huge problem in Malawi is that many people do not have access to clean water. Our denomination likes to locate a borehole near a local United Methodist church and then offer clean water to area residents for free. Each borehole cost about $8,000, and this one was donated in memory of a church member. I saw the kingdom of heaven at the dedication of that borehole in Malawi.

Before this borehole was drilled, the women of this village in the Balaka district had to walk as long as six hours a day to get fresh water. Because of that long distance, villagers often chose shortcuts, drinking the river water, which was closer but unsafe. Many became sick with water-borne diseases. With the completion of the borehole, they could reach clean water in just a few moments. Hundreds of people now had fresh water, not just for drinking and cooking but for washing clothes and bathing. Even the run-off was part of God's miracle! When we arrived, just four months after the borehole was completed, the church had already planted a garden watered by the run-off. The garden offered produce during the dry season when villagers normally could not grow crops.

After a moving service for the dedication of the borehole, we headed back to the small thatched church. Since it was not big enough for all who had gathered, we continued our worship under a tree. Members of our congregation preached and prayed, but more important, the Balaka congregation sang and danced, and the children recited memorized Bible verses in English. Then it came time for a word from the three village chiefs.

Although Christianity is the dominant religion in Malawi, this village was primarily Muslim and had no Christian church before the arrival of the United Methodist Church. The Muslim chiefs, however, had heard that a Christian church in one's village was a good thing and welcomed the United Methodist congregation. Especially with the United Methodist contribution of a borehole and of a year-round garden, they affirmed this Christian group in their midst. The three Muslim chiefs had been known to attend worship services and even to receive communion.

The first chief thanked us for the borehole and asked if we could also build a hospital there. The second Muslim chief apologized for the first chief's bold request and thanked us again for the borehole. The third chief said, "Thank you to our guests for coming and for the borehole." Then he turned to his villagers and said, "To the members of the United Methodist Church in Balaka, I would like to say: Go tell everyone about Jesus and invite them to be part of your church." I thought I'd died and gone to heaven! A Muslim chief was encouraging the people of his village to make disciples for Jesus Christ. If that's not the kingdom come on earth, I don't know what is! Christians and Muslims together inviting people to know the transforming love of Jesus—wow! The kingdom of heaven is like a borehole in Malawi.

Wait …

> As the bridegroom was delayed, all of them became drowsy and slept. (Matt. 25:5)

The itinerary for our 2010 Malawi trip included several days spent touring the churches and projects that the financial giving of our Ankeny church supported. The small village churches were on high alert for us. They told people to show up, looking their best, ready to give us a warm welcome. Only they didn't know exactly when we were coming. The people at one village church thought we would arrive a day earlier than we did. They were ready twenty-four hours in advance, and they waited and waited. Finally, they went home for the night but remained on alert.

The next day when they heard our bus bumping over the rough roads into their remote rural village, people poured from their homes before our eyes and came running to their little thatched roof church, singing and clapping to welcome us. We felt like rock stars or dignitaries! Even though we inadvertently made them wait a whole day for our arrival, they were ready and greeted us with great joy. I think that's how Jesus wants us to live—always expecting that he may be coming around the bend at any moment and having our spiritual lives in order so we're ready to welcome him with great joy.

Radical Hospitality

> Whoever welcomes you welcomes me, and whoever welcomes me welcomes the one who sent me. Whoever welcomes a prophet in the name of a prophet will receive a prophet's reward; and whoever welcomes a righteous person in the name of a righteous person will receive the reward of the righteous; and whoever gives even a cup of cold water to one of these little ones in the name of a disciple—truly I tell you, none of these will lose their reward. (Matt. 10:40–42)

Malawi is called the "warm heart of Africa" with good reason! The people we met on our 2010 church mission trip there were the most welcoming I have ever experienced. Everywhere we went in Malawi, our fellow United Methodist Christians, who have so little in terms of material possessions, welcomed us not just with verbal greetings but with handshakes and hugs, with singing and dancing, and with gifts.

For the women of our group, this welcome often included the gift of a *chitenge*, the colorful wrap-around overskirts worn by most African women. These can be used not just as overskirts but as baby carriers or as head gear to help balance the large loads they carry on their heads. I received four *chitenge* during our short time in Malawi.

For me the most meaningful time was toward the end of our

journey when we were visiting churches on the Balaka circuit. Their pastor spoke little English but wanted us to come to his home to meet his wife. They lived on a narrow street in a small poured concrete home. It had more than one room, which made it above average, but no electricity and probably no running water and not enough furniture for all of us to be seated.

Nonetheless, the pastor's wife, who spoke no English, greeted us as if her home were a palace. With energetic singing and dancing, she enfolded each woman in our group in a *chitenge*, as if to say, "Welcome, friend. You are one of us." I don't know how much those pieces of fabric cost her, but I could tell from the joy on her face that she had received her reward. Welcome is its own reward. That's part of what Jesus is saying in the passage above: "When you welcome others as if you are welcoming me, you experience the presence of God with you." And that is ample reward!

C H A P T E R   6

Prayer

Plain Talk with God

When you are praying, do not heap up empty phrases as the Gentiles do; for they think that they will be heard because of their many words. (Matt. 6:7)

When I was doing hospital social work in the early 1970s, I was privileged to work with a young Roman Catholic sister. She was a couple of years younger than I was and fresh out of college. We were in our early twenties and in our first real jobs. As a lifelong Methodist, I had never known a Catholic nun before and was always somewhat intrigued by my colleague.

One time, I was in charge of a banquet at the local YWCA. I asked my Catholic colleague if she would give the invocation before the meal. I had never heard her pray in public, but I knew she prayed a lot in private. I expected some beautiful, flowery prayer such as might be prayed by Catholic saints from the Middle Ages.

That's not what I got, and I have never forgotten how her prayer that night began. "Well, God," she said, "here we are again, and we're inviting you to be with us." There was nothing flowery about that prayer; it was simple, like someone talking to a loving parent. I wanted to be able to talk to God just like that.

Carried by Prayer

> Do not worry about anything, but in everything by prayer and supplication with thanksgiving let your requests be made known to God. (Phil. 4:6)

In the late 1970s, our journey into ministry took Bob and me from Iowa to seminary in California and then back to pastoral appointments in the United Methodist Church in Iowa. While in California, we worked as student ministry interns at the First Congregational Church, United Church of Christ (UCC), of Oakland. It was our first attempt to see if we could work as a team, and we had a wonderful experience there.

That UCC congregation nurtured and mentored its two young adopted Methodist stepchildren, and when we were ready to return for our first pastoral appointments in United Methodist churches in Iowa, our California congregation did two things I will never forget. The Oakland members wrote personal letters to our Iowa churches, commending us to our new pastorates. That was very kind. And then, more important, they prayed us from California back to Iowa. As we drove across deserts and mountains and plains in our U-Haul truck, with the car hooked up behind and the canoe on top, we felt carried.

They prayed us into our new ministry at Waterloo Grace and Graves United Methodist churches. We can do that for one other— pray that each of us might fulfill the destiny God intends for us.

When Prayer Seems Unanswered

> But I, O Lord, cry out to you; in the morning my
> prayer comes before you. O Lord, why do you cast
> me off? Why do you hide your face from me? (Ps.
> 88:13–14)

I remember a time when I felt my prayers were unanswered.
Bob and I were serving in Waterloo in the 1980s. I was the only one
in the Grace Church office shortly after noon; everyone else had
gone to lunch. I was running late for a speaking engagement at the
University of Northern Iowa in next-door Cedar Falls, where I was
scheduled to address a religion class on the topic "A Typical Day in
Ordained Ministry," when the phone rang. Normally, during the
noon hour I would have let the answering machine take the call.
Besides, I was late. But something said, "Answer the phone."

So I did, and the person on the other end was my younger
brother, John, calling from Kansas City. It was not our custom
to chat long distance over the lunch hour. Besides, my sister-in-
law, Leslie, was in the hospital, fighting for her life against breast
cancer. For the last three years since her mastectomy, we had prayed
fervently for her healing. I'll never forget John's words that day. "Cis,
the doctors say we're losing the battle. Leslie's not going to make it."

Every cell in my body screamed, "No! It can't be. God, are you
listening?" I told my brother, "Oh, John, I'm so sorry," but to God,
I cried out, "Where are you? This is Leslie we're talking about here.
Remember, she leads the children's choir at church (*your* church),
she teaches Sunday school, and she has two daughters to raise. Are
you listening, God?"

After I hung up the phone, I rushed to my car, forgetting my
notes for the UNI class. I drove hurriedly, railing at God all the
way. I parked my car, ran a block or so to the building where the
classroom was located, and up two flights of stairs. The professor
was waiting for me at the door. He'd been worried about my lateness

and probably became more worried when he saw how breathless and distraught I looked. I apologized for being late and entered the classroom. While catching my breath, I simply prayed, "Please teach this class, God. I can't do it right now." I have no idea what I said for the next forty-five minutes, but afterward the teacher, who invited me to speak each year, said, "That was an amazing presentation!"

"Thank you, God," I silently prayed, "but what about Leslie? Her life is so much more important than this."

For a couple of years after Leslie died, my brother raised his two daughters on his own and did a good job. He's a great dad. And then he met a young widow. Her husband had also died of cancer, and she was raising two small sons on her own. Those boys needed a dad, just like my nieces needed a mom. I don't know if it was mere coincidence that brought them together and caused them to fall in love. I like to think it was a God-incidence—a wonderfully surprising answer to all those prayers for healing, not just for one family but for two.

God's answer to our prayers is not always "Here's what you asked for," but I believe it is always "Here I am. No matter what the outcome of this event may be, I am with you. When your loved one dies, when you fail that test you didn't study for, when you lose your job, when your spouse or child or parent or friend lets you down, when you walk through the valley of the shadow of death, I am with you." Thanks be to God.

The Mystery of Healing Prayer

> So I say to you, Ask, and it will be given you; search and you will find; knock, and the door will be opened for you. For everyone who asks receives, and everyone who searches finds and for everyone who knocks, the door will be opened. (Luke 11:9–10)

Around the time of my mother's final illness, I learned some things about the mystery of God's healing. When I was a child growing up, Mom was the greatest! We three kids were the center of her life, and she put us first. I loved my mother deeply, and I prayed fervently for her healing when she was ill.

Unfortunately, Mom didn't take very good care of herself physically. She was a smoker most of her adult life. She suffered from severe headaches, and over the years, she became addicted to the pain medication she took for them. Maybe those factors contributed to her first stroke in her late sixties. I prayed hard for her healing, and she got better for a time, but then she suffered a second stroke that left her unable to walk, or talk very well, or swallow. She required total care at that point and died two years later. I felt like my prayers had not been answered.

Sometimes when our prayers don't seem to be answered, God may simply be saying, "Pay attention. Just watch what I am doing." That was certainly the case with my mother's final illness. God was doing some amazing healing. I just couldn't see it at the time. While Mom and Dad were terrific parents, in their "empty nest" years, they weren't so great as husband and wife. Mom had habits that drove my father crazy, and Dad responded by staying away from home as much as possible. When they were together, they would nag at each other, and when they were apart, they would often call my brothers or me to complain. This went on for a number of years.

Then my mother had her strokes, and after the second one, her extensive care fell to my father. This could have been awful for everyone, but God was listening to our prayers for healing. As I look back on those years, I see that God decided the most important healing was not for my mother's body but for my parents' relationship.

Somehow God reminded my dad of his "in sickness and in health, for better, for worse" marriage vows, and Dad got in touch with his best self. He gave my mother the most beautiful care, and she responded with deep joy and appreciation. In terms of their love for each other, those two years were some of the best they had! God didn't say yes to my prayer for Mom's physical healing but instead channeled that healing energy where God knew it was most needed—in their relationship. So if your prayers are not being answered exactly as you had hoped, step back and pay attention. Perhaps God is doing an even greater thing.

God Provides

> Therefore I tell you, do not worry about your life, what you will eat or what you will drink, or about your body, what you will wear. Is not life more than food, and the body more than clothing? Look at the birds of the air; they neither sow nor reap nor gather into barns, and yet your heavenly Father feeds them. Are you not of more value than they? (Matt. 6:25–26)

We can trust that God is always close at hand working toward our good when we are open to God's provision. For example, God provided for Bob and me when David was about to be born. One of my big worries was what we would do about child care. Like any parents, we wanted to do what was absolutely the best for our child, but I didn't know how to work that out.

God called both Bob and me into full-time ministry, and we didn't have grandparents or other relatives in the area to help out with our newborn. We realized we could stagger our schedules somewhat to be home at different times, but there were still hours each day when we both needed to be working. I didn't know what to do. So I complained to God, "Now look, God, this ministry was your idea, not mine, and if you want me to do it, you've got to help with this child care matter."

Shortly after my prayer of complaint, a church member

approached me and said, "I've been wondering what you are going to do about child care when your baby is born. You see, I have a friend who lives in your neighborhood. She is a licensed day care provider who was thinking about retiring, but she has decided she would like to take care of just one infant next year. Are you interested?"

You bet I was interested! Perhaps it was just a coincidence that for the first year of his life, David ended up with a wonderful grandmotherly day care provider just two blocks from our home, but I'm inclined to think God heard my need and responded. God provides—sometimes in small and coincidental ways—if we make our needs known to God.

Small Prayers Answered

> Rejoice always, pray without ceasing, give thanks in all circumstances; for this is the will of God in Christ Jesus for you. (1 Thess. 5:16–18)

When David was a sophomore, he and a date were going to the high school winter formal dance. The plan was to meet at a friend's home at five-thirty to take pictures of the kids all dressed up, go out for a nice dinner at six-thirty, and on to the dance at eight. At five-twenty-five, as he was ready to walk out the door, I asked David if he had his billfold. He said, "No, and it has my ticket to the dance in it."

We began a one-hour search for the billfold. It was not in the pants David had worn the previous day, in the car, in the coat, under the bed, or tucked between the cushions of any couch or chair in our home. It was not in his high school gym locker or in the car of the friend who had given him a ride home from school. It was nowhere! By this time, David had missed the pictures, but he met the group at the restaurant without billfold or ticket, not knowing if he would be allowed into the dance.

I then went as scheduled to a Christmas concert at church.

While sitting in the sanctuary, I simply prayed, "Dear God, I know you have many more important things to deal with right now, but I could sure use some help finding that billfold." Immediately a voice in my mind said, *You need to look again by the family room couch.* It was such a clear voice that I slipped out of the concert and drove home, telling myself, *Don't be too disappointed if the billfold is not there.* After all, David and I had searched that couch at least twice.

The couch in the family room was a sleeper sofa. I pulled out the bed, got down on my hands and knees, and looked all through the bed frame and the mattress. I was almost ready to give up (again) when I noticed a small dark shadow on the floor beneath the left side of the couch. There was the billfold! I drove to the restaurant and discreetly slipped it to David. I went back to the church concert still in progress, sneaked into a back pew, and said a silent prayer, "Thank you, God, for helping with the little things."

On Our Knees

> For this reason I bow my knees before the Father,
> from whom every family in heaven and on earth
> takes its name. (Eph. 3:14)

I don't usually pray on my knees. Neither does Bob. But if you had stopped by our house on a February day in 2004, you would have found us together kneeling in profound gratitude. We had just received the pathology report after my lumpectomy for breast cancer. The nurse on the phone said, "The margins were clean." Those of you who have also had cancer surgery know this means the surgeon was able to remove the entire cancerous mass. I still had chemotherapy and radiation ahead of me, in case there were cancer cells somewhere else, but at that moment, the message was "So far, so good." And we fell spontaneously to our knees in prayer.

I am well aware that not all cancers can be totally removed or cured, and in this human journey, each one of us will at some point face death. But along the way, all of us also receive countless blessings from God's hands, and when we are attentive to them, sometimes they simply bring us to our knees. I like what the Christian mystic Meister Eckhart once said. "If the only prayer you said in your life was 'Thank You,' that would suffice."[1]

CHAPTER 7

Gifted and Called

Valor

> For God did not give us a spirit of cowardice, but
> rather a spirit of power and of love and of self-
> discipline. (2 Tim. 1:7)

One of the Ward family treasures passed down to Bob is his
great-grandfather's Medal of Honor, awarded for valor during the
Civil War. I've always liked these words from Carl Sandburg: "Valor
is a gift. Those having it never know for sure whether they have it
until the test comes." Here's why that Medal of Honor came to be
awarded to Captain William Henry Ward.

In 1863, while encamped at Milliken's Bend, Louisiana, General
William T. Sherman, commanding the left wing of the Union army
before Vicksburg, decided to try a risky experiment. His plan was
to send supplies to Grant's army, stationed at Grand Gulf, some
fifty miles below, by floating them on barges down the Mississippi
River past the Confederate batteries at Vicksburg. If successful,
this venture would take only eight hours as opposed to a week if
the supplies were sent overland. But it was a dangerous mission, so
volunteers were sought.

On May 3, 1863, Bob's great-grandfather volunteered to command such an expedition under the cover of darkness. The expedition consisted of two large, unwieldy barges loaded with provisions and propelled by a small tugboat securely lashed between the barges. As luck would have it, this was not a dark and cloudy night but the brightest night of the year. At 1 a.m. the Confederates fired upon the captain's expedition, and the Union barges were blown out of the water. A number of men died, with the remainder, including the captain, taken as prisoners of war. They were held for several weeks before being released in a prisoner exchange. The captain returned to Vicksburg in time to see the Confederate surrender there on July 4, 1863. A number of years later, he was awarded the Medal of Honor for valor—not because he had been successful in his mission but because he had been brave and willing to serve.

His experience reminds me that Christ does not call us to success but to service. And sometimes serving takes great courage.

Let Your Light Shine

> You are the light of the world. A city built on a hill cannot be hid. No one after lighting a lamp puts it under the bushel basket, but on the lampstand, and it gives light to all in the house. In the same way, let your light shine before others, so that they may see your good works and give glory to your Father in heaven. (Matt. 5:14–16)

Bob's uncle, Henry Barnett, a retired Presbyterian minister, liked to tell about the summer job he had during college in the 1930s working as a guide in one of the caves in Missouri. He recalled especially taking a group of Boy Scouts through the cave. There were no electric lights strung in the cave, so the guide had a flashlight and all those on the tour carried lighted candles. While in the cave, Henry wanted to give the boys an experience of total darkness, so he asked them to blow out their candles, and he turned off his flashlight. His plan, after a moment of total darkness, was to dramatically sweep his flashlight up in the air, turning it on and proclaiming, "Let there be light!"

However, when Henry swung his flashlight up, it hit the walkway railing, was knocked out of his hand, and fell into the crevices below—and the group remained in total darkness. Contrary to the Boy Scout motto, "Be prepared," no one in the group had a match to relight the candles. As they stood in the darkness, the boys began to panic about how they would get out, and poor Henry became pretty nervous himself. Then he noticed a tiny light. It was coming from the luminous dial on the troop leader's watch. Seizing the watch, Henry held it high above his head, and with that little light he guided the group out of the cave.

You don't have to have a very big light to make a difference in this world if you put your light to work for a good purpose! So let your light shine!

Finding Your Gift May Not Be Easy

> Now there are varieties of gifts, but the same Spirit; and there are varieties of services, but the same Lord; and there are varieties of activities, but it is the same God who activates all of them in everyone. (1 Cor. 12:4–6)

I started taking piano lessons during elementary school. Dad always hoped I could play songs by ear, with all the family gathering round the piano and singing along. So every week I walked a few blocks to the house of a congenial elderly piano teacher for my thirty-minute lesson. Then I would go home and dutifully practice.

By junior high, I had taken to practicing the piano at six in the morning. With all my other activities, this was my only available time. I provided the wakeup call for my family, and I think my brothers resent it to this day!

Regrettably, I was never very good at the piano. Playing didn't come naturally to me, and I had to work at it. My piano teacher, sweet soul that she was, said, "My dear, why don't we try voice lessons? Perhaps your gift is in singing." From then on, I would walk to her house every week and vocalize. I once entered a junior high vocal contest, performing a solo for a team of judges. Suffice it to say, I did not get a one, the highest rating. Sometimes my thoughtful friends would say things like, "I've heard that taking voice lessons can ruin your voice—the strain, you know."

Eventually I gave up voice and piano lessons, accepting the truth that while I enjoy music, I do not have musical gifts. Occasionally while leading worship, I would accidentally leave my microphone on while singing a hymn. Not good! Once when that happened, our director of music came running from the narthex, down the side hall to the back door of the sanctuary, and made frantic signals for me to stop. (Cut your mic quick!)

Let's face it: I do not have—and never will have—musical gifts. But that did not mean God didn't want me to use my voice. It took me until I was around thirty years old to learn the vocal gift God had given to me was not singing but preaching.

A Real Martha

> Now as they went on their way, he entered a certain village, where a woman named Martha welcomed him into her home. She had a sister named Mary, who sat at the Lord's feet and listened to what he was saying. But Martha was distracted by her many tasks; so she came to him and asked, "Lord, do you

not care that my sister has left me to do all the work by myself? Tell her then to help me." But the Lord answered her, "Martha, Martha, you are worried and distracted by many things; there is need of only one thing. Mary has chosen the better part, which will not be taken away from her." (Luke 10:38–42)

For most of my life, I didn't like my name, Martha. While my mother loved the name because it reminded her of the beloved African American woman named Martha who served as her childhood nanny, I thought of my name as a burden. My friends had fun names like Judy and Susie and Jeannie and Kathy, but I was stuck with Martha, a boring name that had no sparkle or pizzazz. It made me think of a plump older woman out in the kitchen baking cookies.

When I was old enough to study the Bible, things got even worse. Consider the story of two sisters, Martha and Mary, close friends of Jesus. One evening, on his way to Jerusalem for the last time, Jesus stopped by their home in Bethany for dinner. No doubt Jesus was tired after his travels, and his heart was probably heavy as he anticipated the final days ahead.

While Mary was quietly sitting at the feet of Jesus, what was Martha doing? Yup, she was out in the kitchen baking cookies and a lot of other food, and Jesus told her she was making too big a fuss. Why didn't she sit down like her sister and listen to his teachings?

That story confirmed for me everything I ever thought about my name. Not only was Martha in the kitchen baking cookies, but she had made the wrong choice, and of all people, it was Jesus who rebuked her. Over the years, whenever people would see me working away on some task and would say, "There's a real Martha," I could feel my shoulders and my jaw tighten, and this little voice within me shout, *It's not my fault that my name is Martha!*

However, eventually I came to terms with my name. I am a Martha through and through. Sometimes I get so frenzied I can hear distinctly in my mind, *Martha, Martha, you worry and fret about so many things. But only one is needful.* I need that reminder. These days I'm generally at peace with my name because I know it need not limit me. Yes, I am Martha, but I can be Mary too. I can put aside my doing and listen to the voice of God. And so can you!

Great Expectations

> He said to him, "'You shall love the Lord your God with all your heart, and with all your soul, and with all your mind.' This is the greatest and first commandment. And a second is like it: 'You shall love your neighbor as yourself.'" (Matt. 22:37–39)

A lesson I learned during my school years is that human beings do their best when great expectations are placed upon them. As a high school student, I was an overachiever. A guidance counselor once pointed out that reality to me in a not-so-helpful way. She said (this is an exact quote), "I don't understand why you make such good grades, Martha, because you aren't that smart. Your standardized test scores aren't very high."

Now if she had had the good sense to ask why I made such good grades despite average test scores, I could have told her. I knew why. It was because of my eighth-grade social studies teacher. In eighth grade, I didn't make exceptionally good grades. I was too busy writing notes to my friends and planning weekend activities, and on one social studies test, I did pretty poorly. As my social studies teacher returned my test, he uttered those fateful words, "Martha, I want to see you after class." I looked at my grade and said, "Yes, sir," and approached his desk after class with fear and embarrassment.

"Your work was very disappointing," he said. "I'm telling you this because I expect you to do much better. You have so many possibilities." As he spoke, his lip quivered with emotion, and I thought perhaps he was going to cry. I have never forgotten his words to me that day or the emotion on his face. Here was a teacher who cared so much about how I did on a social studies test that he got all worked up about it. *Goodness, if he cares so much*, I thought, *maybe I'd better care too.* My academic life was never the same—all because someone cared enough to challenge me to meet higher expectations.

Now consider how much God cares for us. God cares much more than any teacher, friend, or parent, and because of that God expects much from us. That's what the two great commandments are all about—the expectation that we will give our all in loving God and neighbor.

In Deep Water

> When he had finished speaking, he said to Simon,
> "Put out into the deep water and let down your nets
> for a catch." (Luke 5:4)

In 1972, Bob and I moved to Cedar Rapids, Iowa, where Bob had been hired as an associate with an established law firm. Once we had moved into our apartment, it was my turn to seek employment. I was trained as a high school guidance counselor, but no one in Iowa wanted a Kansas-trained guidance counselor with no teaching experience. So I pounded the pavement, looking for work. I was discouraged.

One day I read a local hospital's want ad for a counselor at its patient and family counseling department. Qualifications: a bachelor's degree in social work. I didn't have that degree, but I thought it couldn't hurt to apply. Well, somehow I got the job, and my supervisor must have believed in me, because she threw me into pretty deep water.

She would say, "I am going to turn you into a crisis counselor. There's a family waiting down in the emergency room. The police have just brought in the injured baby, and the parents are suspected of child abuse. Wait with them until the department of human services arrives." Or she might say, "There's a teenager up in pediatrics who tried to take her life. She won't talk to anyone. Go see what you can do." And on it went.

At the time I didn't know why I got that job, but I now understand that God must have known, because the position gave me some of the finest training I could get for my later ministry. Put out in the deep water. You may find, as the disciples did, that God has something great in store for you.

Speak in Public?

> But Moses said to the Lord, "O my Lord, I have never been eloquent, neither in the past nor even now that you have spoken to your servant; but I am slow of speech and slow of tongue." Then the Lord said to him, "Who gives speech to mortals? Who makes them mute or deaf, seeing or blind? Is it not I, the Lord? Now go, and I will be with your mouth and teach you what you are to speak." (Ex. 4:10–12)

The biggest fear for many people is public speaking. I had that fear for many years. I avoided taking speech in high school, but I was required to take a speech class in college. The class included making a short speech in a small room all by myself to a panel of judges. That was one of the most terrifying days of my life! I had prepared my speech on three-by-five cards, and I had practiced forever, but when I stood before those judges, I panicked. My tongue got tied, I tripped over my words, and I had to start over. Finally, I said, "I can't do this," and I rushed from the room. That was failure, and it felt terrible.

While we were living in Cedar Rapids, our pastor asked me

to share the pulpit with two other people on one of his vacation Sundays. Each of us would give a sermonette about five minutes long. I said, "Oh, no, the last thing I could ever do is preach."

Several years later, when it appeared God was calling me to be a preacher, I realized my earlier failure was not the end. It was just a false start, and God would restore me and help me. So, as scary as it was and sometimes still is, I said, "Okay, God, if you want me to speak for you, with your help, I'll try to do my best." I think that's all God asks of us—that we try to do our best.

What Did I Just Say?

> Then Mary said, "Here am I, the servant of the Lord; let it be with me according to your word."
> (Luke 1:38)

Growing up in the United Methodist Church, I never considered pastoral ministry as a vocational choice. I had never seen a woman minister, but I did seem drawn to the helping professions. I thought it would be exciting to be in the Peace Corps, but when my parents suggested something a bit securer, I settled on teaching and trained to be a high school German teacher. While studying for a master's degree in German, I suddenly realized I was more drawn to helping the students than to teaching my subject matter.

I switched to graduate work in guidance and counseling, still planning to work in the public schools. However, I ended up not in public school counseling but with a job doing hospital social work, something I'd never directly studied or contemplated. I enjoyed my work, but it didn't feel like a lifetime career. At the same time, Bob was considering a change in vocation, feeling the practice of law might not be his true calling.

He decided to attend seminary, and when he shared that with me, surprising words came out of my mouth. "I think I'll enroll too," I told him. As soon as the words were uttered, I thought, *Where did that come from? What am I saying?* Like the angel's visit to young Mary of Nazareth, my divinely inspired utterance came as a complete surprise, and I thought, *Who am I to even consider such a thing? I am totally unqualified!*

In the following days, I prayed hard about what I had said and tested the idea with my friends and my colleagues at work. "I think I'm going to seminary to become a United Methodist minister." I expected them to say what my father had said ("What? Have you and that husband of yours gone crazy?"), but instead they responded, "Of course you are. We always thought you would."

Over our years in seminary, I continued pondering this call, wondering what God had in store for me. But it was not until I preached my opening sermon in my first pastoral appointment that I felt that call confirmed. Standing in the pulpit of a small Iowa United Methodist church, I felt a presence. I cannot rightly say it was a voice, but it conveyed the message "Welcome home, daughter." And in my heart, I responded, as young Mary had, "I am a servant of the Lord. Let it be with me according to your word."

No Looking Back

> Jesus said to him, "No one who puts a hand to the
> plow and looks back is fit for the kingdom of God."
> (Luke 9:62)

God calls each one of us to use the talents we have been given for good in the world. Perhaps our call as Christian disciples is more than a polite invitation. Maybe it comes to us with all the urgency of a demand. I first sensed that demand in March 1977.

As seminary students, Bob and I were at the point in our journey toward ordained ministry in the United Methodist Church when we would be interviewed for what was then called "probationary membership" and "deacon's orders." Along with all out-of-state seminarians applying for probationary membership, we were invited to an overnight retreat at Wesley Woods, one of our denomination's camps near Indianola, Iowa. Because I had not grown up in Iowa, I had never been to Wesley Woods. Bob and I were attending the Pacific School of Religion in Berkeley, California, so we got on a plane in San Francisco and flew back to Des Moines.

From the Des Moines airport, for some reason we were instructed to take a bus not to the camp or to Indianola but to an abandoned gas station somewhere between Des Moines and Wesley Woods. The bus left us there, clutching our suitcases and a letter saying two committee members would pick us up. On that chilly March afternoon, we sat on our bags inside the abandoned gas station, and questions arose in our minds. *What are we doing here? What if they never come get us? Is this where the road ends—at an abandoned gas station somewhere in Iowa?* Our twenty-minute wait felt like twenty years, but eventually our ride appeared, and we were off to Wesley Woods.

The probationary interviews were held over a two-day period. As luck would have it, mine was the last interview on the first evening, while Bob's was to be the first of the next morning. To my everlasting gratitude, the interview team approved me, but my excitement was dampened by Bob's strong sense that it was not going to approve him. As he talked about his apprehension, I became more alarmed. He convinced me. Bunking in a cold, rustic cabin at Wesley Woods that night, I got almost no sleep. What if the interview team didn't accept him? What did that mean for our future? What about our dreams of being a ministry team? Was I prepared to pursue this ministry all by myself? It was a long night!

Morning came, and Bob went to his interview. I took a long, prayerful walk—more like a prayer stomp—in the woods. "Okay, God," I finally said impatiently, "you got me here. Now what am I supposed to do?" And immediately my sense of the answer came—not a gentle invitation but a strong demand using words Jesus spoke to his disciples, "Put your hand to the plow. Don't turn back."

Fortunately, Bob's worry was unfounded; his interview team approved him. But for me, that time of uncertainty was pivotal, thrusting me into the position where I could hear God's demand for my life. I was reminded of the line from Isaac Watts's great hymn, "When I Survey the Wondrous Cross," "Love so amazing, so divine, demands my soul, my life, my all."[1]

CHAPTER 8

Powered by the Spirit

Bloom Where You Are Planted

> Happy are those who do not follow the advice of
> the wicked, or take the path that sinners tread, or
> sit in the seat of scoffers; but their delight is in the
> law of the Lord, and on his law they meditate day
> and night. They are like trees planted by streams
> of water, which yield their fruit in its season, and
> their leaves do not wither. In all that they do, they
> prosper. (Ps. 1:1–3)

When we moved from California to our first pastoral
appointments in Iowa, one of the women at the Oakland First
United Church of Christ, where we had served as student interns,
embroidered a picture for us. It showed a large flower growing in a
can of Campbell's tomato soup with the slogan "Bloom Where You
Are Planted." I always suspected she thought living in Iowa was akin
to living in a soup can, but nonetheless, the message of that picture
served us well. Bob and I tried to be the people God needed in each
church and community where we served. Each one of us can bloom

where we are planted, because we are a part of that great force for life, God's Holy Spirit, working in us and through us.

Two by Two

> He called the twelve and began to send them out two by two, and gave them authority over the unclean spirits. (Mark 6:7)

For most of our lives together, Bob and I have been not only partners in marriage but also partners in ministry. We've spent a lot of time together, and we share a number of similarities. We grew up in the same town, our parents knew each other, we went to the same high school and university, we have similar views on many topics, and we enjoy doing many of the same things.

But we also have a number of differences. While in seminary, we took a team position as student interns to discern whether we could work together. At first there were challenges because of our differences. I like to plan ahead; Bob believes in creativity under pressure. I'm very cautious; Bob is a risk taker. Bob likes to envision the big picture; I like to figure out the details. Put those differences in style in one small office with adjoining desks and time pressures of school and work, and occasionally there were rough spots!

However, we also began to notice something more. While our differences were sometimes challenges, they were most often great gifts. Through them we experienced the phenomenon of synergy—that is, as we worked and studied and shared life together, we created an energy that was greater than the sum of the parts. It wasn't that one Bob plus one Martha equaled two people; it was somehow that one Bob plus one Martha was a new entity—Bob 'n' Martha—a partnership that was greater than just one plus one equals two.

On June 12, 1983, we began our first appointment as co-pastors at Waterloo Grace and Graves, and we continued in that form of team ministry until June 29, 2014, when we retired. Here is an excerpt from my part of our 1983 inaugural team sermon.

> Bob and I come before you now, two by two, to celebrate God's Word and to dedicate with you a new model of ministry for these two congregations. 'Two by two,' we come in a new form of team ministry, in excitement and earnestness—not without some anxiety, of course, but with a strong conviction that God is with us all in this new partnership as we seek to enable your discipleship. We say that with confidence because the biblical record makes clear that God endorses the notion of partnership.

For thirty-one years of our thirty-four years in active ministry, we were blessed to serve as co-pastors in the United Methodist Church. We discovered that through the power of the Holy Spirit, there was—and is—a multiplication of energy, insight, and possibility instead of simply addition. We're so grateful Christ sent us out two by two.

Spirit-filled

> When the day of Pentecost had come, they were all together in one place. And suddenly from heaven there came a sound like the rush of a violent wind, and it filled the entire house where they were sitting. (Acts 2:1–2)

We can't see the wind, but we can feel its power! For several years in the early 1980s, Bob and I used red helium-filled balloons as symbols of the wind of Pentecost. We were serving in Waterloo at the time, and Grace United Methodist Church stood proudly at the end of a one-way street. One Pentecost Sunday, at the conclusion of worship, each person was presented with a red helium balloon. We all processed out the front doors of the church and released our balloons into the air as a sign of the Holy Spirit soaring in our midst. It was a beautiful May day, and the balloons rose like a glorious army—beautiful symbols of the power of Christ's church emboldened by the Holy Spirit.

This first balloon launch was so successful that we decided to do the same thing the next year at Pentecost. Worship ended and we all processed out of the church and released our balloons. But that year, Pentecost fell on a muggy, humid day in early June. The air was so heavy that our Pentecost balloons could barely rise. They lifted a bit into the air, and then the sluggish breeze moved them slowly down the street. They looked more like a sulking mob than a glorious army! And I thought, *Sometimes the church is like that—so weighed down by the heaviness of life that our Holy Spirit power is stifled.*

The next year, when Pentecost rolled around, Bob and I were reluctant to give up red helium-filled balloons but decided it was too risky to release them outside. Besides, environmentalists were beginning to explain that helium balloons were a threat to wildlife. So we decided to release the balloons in the sanctuary. They would rise to the majestic ceiling, stay up for twelve hours or so, lose the helium, and come down by Monday. For Sunday worship, this would be a good visual image.

But we made a fatal mistake. We forgot about the ceiling fans, and a number of balloons got caught on them. Their strings got tangled up, and we couldn't get the balloons down. Round and round they went week after week. They lost all their air, and soon they were just limp, pitiful-looking things. And I thought, *Sometimes the church can be like that—limp and lifeless—going around in circles for no good reason.* We had to rent scaffolding to finally get the balloons down.

Fortunately, no balloons were needed on that first Pentecost. Everything those first disciples did was empowered by the mighty wind of the Holy Spirit. They were empowered to preach, to heal, to convert, and to baptize—all through the power of the Spirit. They did amazing things but not under their own power. They were propelled by the wind of the Holy Spirit. May that same Spirit continue to empower the church today!

Small Challenges, Big Spirit

> There is one body and one Spirit, just as you were called to the one hope of your calling, one Lord, one faith, one baptism, one God and Father of all, who is above all and through all and in all. (Eph. 4:4–6)

Following Jesus can take you to interesting places in equally interesting vehicles! In the summer of 1986, a group from Grace Church took a mission trip to the Navajo Nation in Window Rock, Arizona. We traveled in vans, one of which Bob had rented from a place advertising bargain rates. We should have been suspicious about that vehicle when we noticed the right outside rearview mirror was lying on the back seat. Someone at the rental place said, "You aren't hauling a trailer. You won't need it." Once in the vehicle, we noticed a handle on one of the back doors was also missing.

On the way to Arizona, we had a flat tire. The van didn't do well on hills, and we had to replace the air filter and the spark plugs. At one point, while driving home on Interstate 70 in the Rocky Mountains near Vail, Colorado, the van struggled so much that all of us had to get out and walk along the highway. We even had to push at another point. Then, as we drove back across Nebraska, flames started shooting out from under the hood. The fire was out when we opened the hood, but we were still jittery. In fact, as the guys were inspecting the engine, someone took a flash photo, and everybody jumped sky-high. Fortunately, our missioner-mechanics got the van going one more time, and we made it home.

Vehicle woes aside, we had a very meaningful experience in following Jesus as we assisted the Navajo United Methodist congregation to which we were sent. Here is something Bob wrote about the experience in one of his sermons.

> One of the most powerful manifestations of God's presence occurred during a meal we had with the Navajo people. We had just completed a two-hour worship service with them, and it was time for our noon meal. It turned out that it was also time for their noon fellowship coffee time. As we both entered the fellowship hall where we were staying and had prepared our meal, it was clear that the appropriate thing to do was to invite them for lunch. We did not know how we were going to feed thirty extra people, but fifteen missioners went into the small kitchen in an effort to multiply the loaves and fishes. They were successful, and a wide variety of food was set out, which proved more than adequate for everyone's appetites.

> Before we ate, we paused to say grace, and joining around the table of food which God had provided for us, we sang, "We are one in the Spirit, we are one in the Lord, and we pray that all unity will one day be restored." It was clear to me and others that the infinite and eternal home which God's love gives to all those who will accept it had taken the place of our physical homes, which we had left so far behind. It is on the journey, when one has left one's physical home, when one experiences the universal spiritual presence of God, which makes all places safe and secure.

A second thing which we experienced on the journey was the powerful uniting influence of a common purpose—God's purpose. Because of that shared purpose to which we had been called, whenever situations arose which threatened to disrupt that purpose, from van breakdowns to unexpected meals, we pulled together and rose to the occasions. One instance which stands out occurred when we were laying 140 feet of sidewalk from the parsonage to the church. It was really hot outside, and we had never done this kind of work before. We had to carry all the cement in buckets by hand, but somehow, working together we accomplished our goal.

On our mission trip, the most important thing was not all the concrete we poured or how many times our bargain van broke down. The important thing was the spirit of Christian unity that we felt as a group and that we shared with our Navajo sisters and brothers.

Igniting the Pilot Light

When the day of Pentecost had come, they were all together in one place. And suddenly from heaven there came a sound like the rush of a violent wind, and it filled the entire house where they were sitting. Divided tongues, as of fire, appeared among them, and a tongue rested on each of them. All of them were filled with the Holy Spirit and began to speak in other languages, as the Spirit gave them ability. (Acts 2:1–4)

What is the Holy Spirit? Some have used the analogy of a pilot light on a furnace or a stove. The spark of the divine is always present within us, but it needs something to ignite it. Such an analogy brings to mind the old boiler at Grace Church in Waterloo.

The church had been built in 1897. I don't think the boiler was quite that old, but it was a big cast iron monster that seemed ancient to me. Except for the secretary, Bob and I were the only staff at the church, so one of our Saturday night tasks during winter was to go to the church to turn up the heat for Sunday morning.

Most often that meant simply adjusting the thermostat, but sometimes the old boiler would not automatically fire up. Then we would have to go down to the basement to stoke the boiler. Whenever this task fell to me, I had a terrible fear I would blow up the building. As I remember, we had to turn a dial, pull a lever, and open the small door revealing the pilot light so it could get some air. If we did all that just right, it would go "Whoosh!" A great fire would fill the inside of the boiler, and we'd have power!

How's your spiritual life? If it seems a little cool or lukewarm, maybe it's time to journey down into your inner life a bit to stoke that spark of the Holy Spirit so it will burst into flame. Perhaps you will experience what theologian Pierre Teilhard de Chardin described: "Someday, after mastering the winds, the waves, the tides and gravity, we shall harness for God the energies of love, and then, for a second time in the history of the world, man will have discovered fire."[1] Whoosh!

Following the Spirit's Lead

> So the word of the Lord grew mightily and prevailed.
> Now after these things had been accomplished, Paul
> resolved in the Spirit to go through Macedonia and
> Achaia, and then to go on to Jerusalem. He said,
> "After I have gone there, I must also see Rome."
> (Acts 19:20–21)

In the Acts of the Apostles, Luke records how Paul and the disciples sometimes changed their direction upon the urging of the Holy Spirit. That happened to me one day in 2006. I was taking the slow way from downtown Des Moines back to Ankeny after making hospital calls. I was traveling north on Second Avenue and thinking about our church's involvement in outreach and mission.

Ankeny First United Methodist Church is a large suburban church. Given its many members and resources, I was always praying that God would guide us in how best to share with those in need. When I had neared College Avenue in Des Moines, it was as though the Holy Spirit said, "Turn left to Trinity United Methodist Church before returning to Ankeny." The impulse was so strong that I instinctively turned the car left and drove to that church.

Trinity was an inner-city church with a small membership but a big commitment to urban mission. At that time, Trinity shared ministry with the nonprofit agency Children and Family Urban Movement and with a Latino United Methodist congregation, Las Americas. When I arrived at the church, both the Las Americas pastor and the Trinity pastor were in. I told them, "I'm here because I believe Christ wants us to explore how our Ankeny congregation can be in greater ministry partnership with all the urban ministries here at Trinity." We had an exciting conversation, and I returned to Ankeny. The following Sunday in worship I told our congregation, "I believe Christ is calling us to be more involved in the ministries at Trinity. If anyone would like to consider this, please come to a meeting next week."

We scheduled the meeting in a small room in the church's lower level, but on the night of the meeting, we had to relocate to the larger fellowship hall because so many people came. From that starting point, our ministries with Trinity grew in a variety of ways: serving the Children and Family Urban Movement's supper club twice a month, helping with the breakfast club, doing minor building improvements, cultural sharing with the Las Americas congregation, attending each other's worship, teaching in English

Language Learner (ELL) classes, providing a Christmas party for ELL families, providing ELL child care, consulting on Trinity capital campaigns, becoming official mission partners with Trinity, and giving 5 percent of Ankeny's capital campaign proceeds to its projects.

A Trinity church member once told me, "Hardly a day goes by that there is not someone from Ankeny First UMC in our building helping our ministries." Ankeny First's involvement was beneficial to Trinity, but it had an equal impact on those from Ankeny who volunteered at Trinity. One Ankeny member put it like this: "Our partnership with Trinity has brought our family together to serve, and I know it has left an imprint on our children, planting seeds for life." Of all the ways I served at Ankeny, connecting our suburban congregation with this inner-city congregation was perhaps the most clearly Spirit-led.

CHAPTER 9

Faith and Feelings

Stubborn Me

> When I was a child, I spoke like a child, I thought like a child, I reasoned like a child; when I became an adult, I put an end to childish ways. For now we see in a mirror, dimly, but then we will see face to face. Now I know only in part; then I will know fully, even as I have been fully known. And now faith, hope, and love abide, these three; and the greatest of these is love. (1 Cor. 13:11–13)

I had a childhood friend named Susie. We were destined to be close friends because our mothers were best friends and we were born a week apart. We played together and celebrated our birthdays together, but we did not always get along. I remember one afternoon in particular when we were around six years old. We were playing dress-up at Susie's house. Using her mother's old party dresses and high heels, we were having a grand time pretending we were princesses or movie stars or other glamorous characters.

Then we argued about something. I don't remember what. Susie did something that made me mad, and I wasn't about to forgive her.

Finally, she said, "Hey, I get my way because this is my house." I responded with what I thought was the ultimate threat, "Well, then I'll just go home." To my surprise, she said, "I dare you."

So I ripped off my princess dress, put on my own clothes, and stormed out the door, frowning all the way. *I'll never be her friend again*, I thought. I had stomped about one block when I realized I wasn't sure of my way home. Susie's family lived about two miles from my house, and my mother always drove me. I knew the general direction home, but that was it. However, I was not about to go back and let Susie win the day, so I angrily marched off toward my house.

Susie was sure I was just bluffing, so she didn't immediately tell her mother I had left. As I walked on, my anger turned first to worry and then to fear. While I thought I was going the right way, I was never very good with directions. But there was no way I was going back. My fear had me in tears, but my childish stubbornness kept my feet on their foolish journey.

I did not get all the way home before my panicked, angry, but greatly relieved mother found me. I don't remember if I was punished or if just seeing how much I had worried her was punishment enough. I had gone from wearing the garments of a make-believe princess to putting on the real-life accessory of a stubborn spirit, which led me to do something that was foolish and dangerous. Ever since, I've tried not to let my stubbornness or anger cause me to do childish things, remembering that our faith calls us to the higher path of love.

Failure Isn't the End

> Therefore I am content with weaknesses, insults, hardships, persecutions, and calamities for the sake of Christ; for whenever I am weak, then I am strong. (2 Cor. 12:10)

One of my least favorite childhood memories is of the fifth-grade spelling bee. All three fifth-grade classes at our school came together for this special end-of-the-year event. We students formed a big circle around the perimeter of the classroom, and the teacher progressed around the circle asking each of us to spell a word. The desks were pushed into the middle of the room, and students sat down after they had missed a word.

My turn came, and I was excited and a little nervous. I don't remember what the word was, but I misspelled it and had to sit down. I was the first of about sixty fifth-graders to sit down in the middle of the room. It may have been just minutes before another student misspelled a word, but it seemed like hours to me as I sat there all alone. Each successful speller smiled smugly at me, no doubt thinking, *Too bad you can't spell.*

We all have areas in life where we are weak, but thank goodness we do not have to rely exclusively on our own strength. As the children's song "Jesus Loves Me" says, "We are weak, but he is strong. Yes, Jesus loves me." I became an above-average speller, but more important, I learned in the fifth grade that one failure is not the end. With Christ by our side, we can triumph over life's challenges, both big and small.

Loving Intimate Enemies

> But I say to you, Love your enemies and pray for those who persecute you. (Matt. 5:44)

I was thinking about enemies one year around Valentine's Day, a day when we sometimes give symbols of our love. I wondered if we send valentines to our enemies—not our faraway enemies, whom we may hate in the abstract, but our intimate enemies, those we dislike up close. Do you have any of those?

I can't think of any such enemies as an adult, but when growing up, I was a little clearer on this subject. I had at least two intimate enemies, my brother Bob, who was eleven months older than I was, and my brother John, who was three years younger. Like most brothers and sisters, we were from time to time arch enemies, and because there were two of them and only one of me, I sometimes felt picked on.

Maybe it was the way our house was laid out. My bedroom was at the very back of the house, and the only exit was through my brothers' room. For some diabolical reason, the lock to my bedroom was on their side of the door. Sometimes, just to be mean, my brothers would lock my door and then go about their business, with me unknowingly locked in.

I would pound and pound on my door, yelling until one of them would approach and ask smugly, "Anything wrong, Cis?" They were lucky at those moments that there was a door between us! I treasure my good adult relationship with my brothers, but when I was a child, an expression of my feelings occasionally might have been "I hate you."

Have you noticed how often those words are spoken in our homes or are acted out in our most intimate relationships? And yet Jesus said, "Love your enemies." My brothers and I were fortunate to grow into that love as we matured, but some families carry an intimate enmity all their lives. If that's true for you, perhaps some serious conversation with the One who loves us all can begin your healing.

When You Want to Hide

> At that place he came to a cave, and spent the night there. Then the word of the Lord came to him, saying, "What are you doing here, Elijah?" (1 Kings 19:9)

When Elijah was running from evil Queen Jezebel, he hid

in a cave. A cave is a safe place to hide. In fact, I've done that myself! Caves were an important part of my growing up. With two grandparents (Mamo and Papo) who became spelunkers and cave owners in their retirement, my brothers and I spent lots of time in caves, especially in the family-owned commercial one—Bridal Cave—at the Lake of the Ozarks in Missouri. We often stayed in my grandparents' lake home near the cave, but I learned early on that if dangerous weather was brewing in the area—thunderstorms, tornadoes, strong winds—the place to go was the cave. There was no better spot. In there I would be safe and secure.

At night when the thunder rumbled and the wind picked up, my mother was always the first to say, "I think it's time to go to the cave." My father usually scoffed at the idea, saying, "The storm will blow over."

"All right," my mother would say. "Do as you like, but I'm going to the cave."

"Me too!" came the response from my brothers and me, and we would traipse to the cave, peering cautiously from the entrance. The rain pounded and the wind whistled outside but left us untouched. I know what it's like to hide in a cave.

I also know we sometimes hide in caves in a figurative sense when we retreat from life because it seems too scary or too overwhelming. I am inclined to want to hide if I think a task is too big or the risks are too great. Sometimes I would like to hide in a cave if I think people will make fun of me or put me down. Sometimes I want to hide because I am tired or discouraged.

Such hiding may be okay for a short respite, but during such times, if we stop the turmoil in our minds long enough to listen, we will hear God asking, "What are you doing in there?" And if we continue listening after we have made our excuses, perhaps we, like Elijah, will hear God's call on our lives.

Envy Can Make You Sick

> Rid yourselves, therefore, of all malice, and all guile,
> insincerity, envy, and all slander. (1 Peter 2:1)

Have you ever felt envious of another person? I have. The person I envied most as a teen was my friend Susie, whom I mentioned in my earlier reflection on stubbornness. Susie and I didn't exactly choose each other as friends; we were assigned to be friends by our mothers, who were best friends and managed to give birth to us just one week apart. Even though we hadn't picked each other, we remained good friends as we grew up. We chose to be roommates as freshmen in college, and Susie was a bridesmaid in my wedding. We kept in touch over the years until she died in her sixties of leukemia. I never told Susie I envied her. That's one of the characteristics of envy—it's often a secret sin.

I envied Susie because she was thin. Our culture tells girls and women that thin is beautiful. That was as true when I was a girl as it is today. When I was growing up, no one would accuse me of being thin, so I was envious of my friend. In the eighth grade, when Susie and her family moved to another city, I was distraught for some time. In retrospect, I think her departure during our teen years gave me the distance I probably needed to develop a healthy self-image.

Had Susie remained close by, I might have been more vulnerable to some of the eating disorders that plague young women today—anorexia, bulimia—because envy makes you sick. That's why we use the expression "green with envy." I think Shakespeare called envy "a green-eyed monster"[1] because he knew the great damage that can be done by this sin-sickness.

Over time, I came to see that my friend Susie had a few more struggles in her life than I ever had to face. God gently helped transform my envy into empathy. Perhaps that is God's goal for all of us.

Good Anger Management

> Be angry but do not sin; do not let the sun go down
> on your anger, and do not make room for the devil.
> (Eph. 4:26–27)

Early in our marriage, Bob and I purchased one of those Bozo the Clown punching bags. When we were irritated with each other or angry about something outside of our relationship, we would put Bozo between us and knock him back and forth. Bozo would pop right up for more, and we would pound on him until we were worn out or we collapsed in a fit of laughter. And sometimes we found that after we had released the anger, it simply went away, or we could deal with it in a rational way. "Get the anger out," says the apostle Paul. "Get rid of it. Don't let the sun set on it."

Giving Up Fear for Lent

> He called the crowd with his disciples, and said
> to them, "If any want to become my followers, let
> them deny themselves and take up their cross and
> follow me." (Mark 8:34)

In 2004, at the evening Ash Wednesday service, I offered this meditation.

> Ashes, a symbol of our mortality. I confess to
> you tonight that I have been considering my own
> mortality more than usual these days. It has been
> ten days since I received a diagnosis of breast cancer.
> Cancer. Many of you have faced that diagnosis
> yourselves or in your family, and you know that it
> leads a person to ask scary questions that are largely
> unanswerable. I feel fortunate that my cancer was

detected on a mammogram, and that a week from Friday I will have surgery, and that after surgery there will be some treatment options to fight this disease.

Nonetheless, I enter this Lenten season with a depth of personal concern which is much greater than I would choose. We Protestants have generally not taken this notion of giving up something for Lent very seriously, but if you choose to do so, I would invite you not necessarily to give up some food or something else external but rather to give up an attitude that keeps you from following Jesus, like worry, fear, or anxiety about the future. Is there something in your life which weighs heavily upon you and frightens you? The attitude I want to give up for Lent is fear. You see, I'm a pretty scared person right now.

As I await surgery, I feel like a walking time bomb, and Bob and I have asked ourselves all those scary questions which have no answers. Over the last twenty years, we have walked the path of life-threatening illness with many people, including a number of you. Now we walk the path ourselves, and I'm afraid—not of the surgery, not of the follow-up treatments, but of this horrible sneaky disease called cancer.

So I know what I need to give up for Lent this year. I need to give up fear and open myself to the great peace that comes from walking with Christ, and I need your prayers to help me do that. Maybe you have some attitude like that which you need to give

up this season. Let your church family help you do
that. Let's walk together on this journey with Jesus.

Left to ourselves, I suppose none of us would be able to journey
with Jesus. Though it leads to abundant life, the path seems far too
hard. Luckily, we do not have to do it by ourselves. We are invited to
make that journey together, assured that God will show us the way.
To take up the cross and to follow Jesus, there may be something
each of us must put down first—a burden, an attitude, a heartache.
Let us find courage and strength and always remember we do not
journey alone.

CHAPTER 10

Christian Community

We Are Nurtured in Community

> Blessed are those who trust in the Lord, whose trust is the Lord. They shall be like a tree planted by water, sending out its roots by the stream. (Jer. 17:7–8)

I love trees! A hike in the woods puts me as close to heaven as I can be on earth. When I was a child, my grandfather Krehbiel (Papo, we called him) planted a little evergreen tree for me—and one for each of my brothers—beside my grandparents' first cabin on the Lake of the Ozarks. Every summer the first thing we would do upon arrival at the cabin was check on our trees to see how they had grown. My tree was soon taller than I was.

As time went by, my grandparents sold that small cabin and bought a lake home at another location, so I didn't see the tree anymore. Then one summer, probably twenty-five years later, when Bob and I were vacationing at the Lake of the Ozarks, I said, "Let's take a boat ride to the old cabin. I want to check on my tree." When we got there, we noticed the current owner had expanded the cabin, though luckily not in the direction of my tree. However, when I went to see it, I found not the three trees planted for me and my brothers but a whole grove of beautiful, strong trees. I couldn't tell which one was mine.

Initially, I was sorry I couldn't identify "my tree," because it seemed to carry some part of my childhood with it. But then I thought, *No. This grove is good. These trees have nurtured one other. Together they have grown strong and healthy.*

The church is like a grove of trees planted by the water. We may start out with an individual planting of faith, but as we grow, the church community is a place where we can mature together—rooted in God and yet feeling the love and support of one another.

Always Part of the Body

> If the foot would say, "Because I am not a hand, I do not belong to the body," that would not make it any less a part of the body. (1 Cor. 12:15)

Back in the sixties, my father had a disagreement with one of the pastors at my parents' church. The pastor never knew it, but he angered my father one Sunday. Dad thought the young associate pastor's corporate prayer of confession was too political, so Dad got up and walked out of worship. The prayer probably *was* too political. It was the time of the Vietnam War and of the antiwar movement. That young pastor could have learned something if Dad had visited with him.

But Dad stopped attending. He still belonged and gave financially to the church, but for thirty years he didn't attend. Fortunately, the church did not forget about him. The staff continued to send my parents correspondence, and when my mother became ill, the visitation pastor called on her regularly. Another of the pastors ministered to our family at the time of her death and did a fine job with her funeral.

Just because one part of the body of Christ is out of joint doesn't mean that part gets amputated. I was glad when, after Mom's death, Dad started attending worship at that church again. He liked the informal Saturday night service in the church gym. And when he died, my brothers and I felt good about designating his memorial gifts to the church. It was one way we could thank the body for having the grace to stay connected.

I Get By with a Little Help from My Friends

> Peter answered him, "Lord, if it is you, command
> me to come to you on the water." He said, "Come."
> So Peter got out of the boat, started walking on the
> water, and came toward Jesus. (Matt. 14:28–29)

I don't like taking risks. For example, in the early 1970s, Bob and I were backpacking in the mountains with another couple, our close friends. In June there was still melting snow in the higher elevations. At one point, our path crossed a large patch of snow, and right in the middle of the snow a fairly significant stream was flowing rapidly down the mountain.

Because of the snow, I couldn't see exactly where the stepping-stones were in that fast-moving stream, and I was sure I would miss one and be carried down to the bottom of the mountain. There was no way I was going to cross that snowy stream! I wouldn't have been like the apostle Peter either. No way would I have gotten out of the boat!

However, to continue our backpacking trip, we had to cross that stream. Finally, my three hiking partners got out a length of rope, which we tied around our waists, and I walked gingerly across the steam, roped to the others to keep me from being swept into oblivion. I don't like to take risks, but sometimes Jesus calls us out of the boat, out of our comfort zone. That's when I'm grateful for my companions in the church who walk with me in that venture.

Small Group, Large Blessing

> So then you are no longer strangers and aliens, but you are citizens with the saints and also members of the household of God, built upon the foundation of the apostles and prophets, with Christ Jesus himself as the cornerstone. In him the whole structure is joined together and grows into a holy temple in the Lord; in whom you also are built together spiritually into a dwelling place for God. (Eph. 2:19–22)

In the years before we left for seminary, Bob and I were part of a small group for young couples at our church. We called ourselves the Around Thirties. At one point the group studied the book *The Edge of Adventure*, by Keith Miller and Bruce Larson.[1] It is probably outdated today, but back then it was just the right book for young adults trying to decide how to be Christian in the workplace and the community.

The book was good, but the small-group discussion was even better. I learned so much from that group! For one thing, I learned that in Christ, many of the measures used by society simply don't matter. At the time, Bob was practicing law with a long-established firm. As an associate in that firm, he was expected to socialize with people of high standing in the community. That was okay, but in our small group, there were people from many social levels. Some had advanced college degrees, others had high school diplomas, some had high-paying jobs, and a few were struggling after being laid off. Further, we were both Republicans and Democrats; some people had brilliant insights and quick wits, while others were slow to speak and had common wisdom. However, all were a part of this wonderful entity called the body of Christ, and I learned from each one of them. We laughed and cried together, and this small group encouraged Bob and me as we took our leap into ministry.

Over the years, we kept in touch with some of the Around Thirties, and on our first Sunday preaching in Ankeny in 2000, we recognized two faces in the congregation from our group so many years earlier. Now living nearby, they had been tracking our journey in ministry and had come that morning to encourage us in our next step. It felt like we were family—members of the household of God.

The Family of God

> O Lord, you have searched me and known me. You know when I sit down and when I rise up; you discern my thoughts from far away. You search out my path and my lying down, and are acquainted with all my ways. Even before a word is on my tongue, O Lord, you know it completely. (Ps. 139:1–4)

Have you ever wondered where you fit in or where you really belong? I didn't feel like I had found my place in life until I was in my thirties. I'd enjoyed childhood and my school years, and by age twenty-two, I was happily married, but vocationally I had not yet found where I belonged.

When Bob and I were a married couple in our late twenties, our search for belonging led us to seminary in Berkeley, California. We enjoyed our time in the San Francisco Bay area, but when our studies were completed, we were ready to return to the Midwest. Like other United Methodist seminarians, we eagerly awaited a call informing us of our appointment to local churches in Iowa. The call never came. We finally made the appropriate Iowa contact, only to be told, "Oh, no, you're not coming back. You're staying in California." That was news to us! After we affirmed our intent to return, our Iowa contact said, "Well, we're almost done with appointments, and we're really at the bottom of the barrel, but we'll see what we can do."

A few weeks later we were contacted and offered appointments to serve two churches in Waterloo. We knew we'd better say yes because there were no alternatives. The small church to which I was being appointed was described as an angry, hurting congregation that could benefit from the kind of "nurture" I could give. What I didn't learn at the time was that members had often complained about their previous pastor. In fact, they had been pretty forceful—even rude— about it. The superintendent had become irritated with them and had said, "Well, if you're going to be that way about it, we'll just send you a woman pastor."

As you might imagine, I felt some apprehension on my first Sunday in the pulpit, and the small congregation felt plenty of it too. And yet there was in that little sanctuary a presence greater than any of our fears, and I knew I belonged—not to a particular church, not to a particular place, but as one set aside for a particular role in the family of God.

Catching Fish—or Not

> As Jesus passed along the Sea of Galilee, he saw Simon and his brother Andrew casting a net into the sea—for they were fishermen. And Jesus said to them, "Follow me and I will make you fish for people." And immediately they left their nets and followed him. As he went a little farther, he saw James son of Zebedee and his brother John, who were in their boat mending the nets. Immediately he called them; and they left their father Zebedee in the boat with the hired men, and followed him. (Mark 1:16–20)

As young adults, Bob and I once went canoeing in the Canadian Boundary Waters as part of a vacation. We didn't go with a group. It was just the two of us, and we had a great time. The lakes were beautiful; the camping was great; the portages with our canoe weren't too difficult. The only thing that was not so great was the fishing. Our luck was terrible!

For several days we paddled out in the lake at what we thought was the right time to fish and threw out our lines. Then we would wait and wait and wait. Fish would be jumping all around us, but not a single one would bite at our hooks. Other people were fishing near us and catching fish like mad. We became terribly envious! Every time they would move their canoes away from the place they'd been fishing, we'd paddle over in desperate hope that there were still some fish for us. But no. We didn't catch a single fish the whole time we were there.

Now that wouldn't have been so horrible except that we had planned on eating fish for lunch and dinner, and accordingly we had packed no provisions other than instant oatmeal for breakfast. In fact, we had a lot of oatmeal because I thought we might be hungry in the mornings and would want more than one packet each. So we had instant oatmeal for breakfast—and instant oatmeal for lunch and instant oatmeal for dinner. And we've never been too crazy about instant oatmeal since then.

At a meeting, we were once asked during the get-acquainted time to share our favorite season. One woman said there were only two seasons in her family—fishing and non-fishing. "Wow, we'd be in trouble there," I reflected, but later I thought maybe that was a good way to describe how we live out our Christian commitment. Are we in a season of fishing or of not fishing? Reaching out with the love of Jesus may not always yield immediate, visible results. Sometimes it's hard work, but it's a lot more interesting than sitting on the shore eating oatmeal!

Faithful Footsteps in the Snow

> I have fought the good fight, I have finished the
> race, I have kept the faith. From now on there is
> reserved for me the crown of righteousness, which
> the Lord, the righteous judge, will give me on that
> day, and not only to me but also to all who have
> longed for his appearing. (2 Tim. 4:7–8)

One Sunday morning in the 1980s we had a terrible snowstorm in Waterloo, Iowa. Bitter high winds accompanied deep snow. Nothing in town was moving on that January morning, so we canceled worship and Sunday school, putting the word out over radio. Later, after the plows had gone through, Bob went to Grace Church to check on the building. He found two small sets of footprints leading up to the door. He soon learned they belonged to two saintly women in their eighties. These faithful followers had made their way across town through heavy snow to Sunday school, only to find the church doors locked. After that, we adopted a policy never to cancel worship, no matter how bad the roads got (unless law enforcement told everyone not to go out). The folks in our subsequent congregations didn't quite understand our conviction, but we always thought, *If those elderly saints could make it, so can we!*

A Silent Well of Strength

> Is there no balm in Gilead? Is there no physician
> there? Why then has the health of my poor people
> not been restored? (Jer. 8:22)

My sister-in-law, Leslie Dalton, died of breast cancer when she was only forty years old. Leslie fought a courageous and amazingly hopeful battle against cancer, and even though the disease took her life, I know that in the eyes of God, she triumphed because of the impact she had on the lives of all who knew her. A while back I came across a letter she had written us about a year before she died.

She wrote, "On the emotional side I am so grateful that I've always had a strong faith in God, because it has really gotten me through these months. I think I have always taken my church background and involvement for granted, but in this crisis, it has been like a silent well of strength to draw from."

There is a balm in Gilead—the power of God in Christ to give us hope in all circumstances—and that hope is best found in community. Perhaps some can find hope in God in isolation, but for most of us hope is made real in human community. We do not have to face trying times alone but can come to our church family where we will find a community of hope.

More Than a Superficial Faith

> Not everyone who says to me, "Lord, Lord," will enter the kingdom of heaven, but only the one who does the will of my Father in heaven. (Matt. 7:21)

Knoxville, Iowa, is sometimes called the Sprint Car Capital of the World. In the seven years we served in ministry there, Bob and I experienced the phenomenon of the Sprint Car Nationals, a week when persons from all across the world came to our town of eight thousand people to watch sprint car races. During the 1998 Nationals, I did something I'd never done before: I bought one of the event's signature T-shirts with pictures of neon-colored sprint cars. I bought one for our nine-year-old son, David, too. After living in Knoxville for six years, it seemed like the right thing to do.

Then I decided to find out whether people thought I was a sprint car fan just by virtue of my T-shirt. One evening shortly before the races began, I put on my race T-shirt and walked with Bob and

David several blocks down the highway to the Sprint Car Hall of Fame. And guess what? People thought I was a race fan. I looked just like them!

But then it happened. Someone stopped and asked me a question—not a Knoxville question but a racing question. I didn't even understand the question, much less know the answer! Just wearing a T-shirt doesn't make you a fan. You have to go to the races, you have to understand the races, and you have to care about the races.

Likewise, just saying you're a Christian doesn't mean you are one. You can walk up and down the street around a church and look like a Christian, but until you go inside, until you begin to study the Christian faith, and until you try to live out your faith in the world, appearances don't mean much. There's more to faith than that.

Keep Growing

> We must no longer be children, tossed to and fro and blown about by every wind of doctrine, by people's trickery, by their craftiness in deceitful scheming. But speaking the truth in love, we must grow up in every way into him who is the head, into Christ, from whom the whole body, joined and knit together by every ligament with which it is equipped, as each part is working properly, promotes the body's growth in building itself up in love. (Eph. 4:14–16)

In Bob's childhood home, his parents used a basement door frame to mark the height of Bob and of his twin brother, Bill, as they grew up. Living in church parsonages over the years, we couldn't keep track of our son David's growth that way, so I was glad in 1994 when we picked up a growth chart at the Iowa State Fair. David was only three feet eleven at the time. He topped off that chart by about 1999, and now he's six feet tall.

It's pretty easy to measure growth in terms of height—until we get older. We reach our maximum height by young adulthood. We hold that a while, and then some of us start shrinking. All my adult life, I'd been five feet six but no longer. The last time my height was measured, I was only five feet five. I'm shrinking.

Just like we can measure our children's physical growth by their height, we can also fairly easily measure their growth in other areas—academics, social skills, music, athletics. We can even see their growth in faith through their involvement in Sunday school, confirmation, and youth programs.

But as we get older, growth tends to get a little more difficult to measure, and that's true for our growth in faith as well. Sometimes we stop going to Sunday school; we may occasionally volunteer in the church, but many of us are not involved in any regular, ongoing study or reflection that would help us to grow in faith. That has made me wonder: could we be shrinking in our faith?

The Christian faith isn't something you graduate from when you complete confirmation or high school or when your children are grown and you're no longer a Sunday school teacher or a youth helper. God isn't done with us whether we're in or out of school. Quite the opposite is true. God expects us to keep growing all of our lives.

Faith Is an Action Word

> What good is it, my brothers and sisters, if you say
> you have faith but do not have works? (James 2:14)

My brother Bob is just a year older than I am and lives in Denver. When his wife, Lynda, died suddenly in June 2012, he went through the intense grief that comes with losing a life partner.

During this time, he stayed closely connected to his church, Trinity United Methodist, a large, historic church in downtown Denver.

On a late summer Sunday, my brother was driving to worship when he noticed that many downtown Denver streets were closed with barricades. The USA Pro Cycling Challenge was about to begin in that area, and every approach to my brother's church appeared to be blocked. Finally, he noticed an officer by a traffic barricade and pulled over to explain his predicament. "I'm just trying to get to church," Bob said. Fortunately, the officer responded, "That sounds like a really good reason for me to move this barricade."

When my brother arrived at church, it appeared that most members had given up trying to get through the barricades. The massive sanctuary was almost empty. Bob could see none of the people he had been sitting with in recent weeks, so for the first time since her death, he decided to return to the pew where he and his wife had frequently sat. Because of the low attendance, Bob was the only one in that pew. As the service began, my brother felt so alone and awful that he thought, *I should have turned around at the barricades and gone home.*

The congregation stood to sing the opening hymn, and suddenly another member stepped in beside my brother, gave him a big hug, and started singing with him. "Where's your family?" Bob asked.

"Oh, they're in the balcony because the kids are wiggly," the friend said.

"Shall we move up there?" my brother asked.

"No," said the friend. "I want to sit right here with you."

That friend put his faith into action that morning. He looked around with the eyes of Jesus and noted, "There's someone who is very lonely and sad," and then went to be with him.

My brother has a great singing voice. He's always enjoyed singing in church. After the service, a man he had not met introduced himself. "I'm in the choir," he said, "and *you* should be in the choir. You have a great voice and we need you. Besides, we're like family to each other." That member also put his faith into action. He was alert to the gifts of another person and invited him to use them. This was not the first time my brother had been invited to join the choir. It was probably the fifth time, but it was the right time! And my brother was at choir practice the following Wednesday.

When my brother called to tell me this story, he said, "I am so glad I went to church today. Just think of what I would have missed if I hadn't come." When I told him I wanted to tell his story in my sermon, he said, "If I were telling the story, I'd call my experience 'Must be present to win'!" Christ touched him that day not through the preacher or the worship service but through the people of that congregation who looked around their sanctuary with Jesus's eyes and put their faith into action.

CHAPTER 11

The Cycle of Life

Waiting

> Then Mary said, "Here am I, the servant of the
> Lord; let it be with me according to your word."
> (Luke 1:38)

In 1988 when Bob and I were expecting our son's birth, we asked the question every couple asks: "What is the due date? When will this baby most likely be born?" The doctor replied, "December 25, Christmas Day." Mercifully, David waited until December 27 to arrive, but we were awestruck by the possibility that our child might be born on the day we celebrate the birth of Jesus. I spent a good deal of time during those nine months reflecting on all the ways in which my pregnancy was alike or different from Mary's. In fact, I wrote a poem about my inner journey. I called it "An Advent Prayer."

She was about fourteen,
this young Mary who would
bear the Christ.
I am forty-one,
old enough to be her mother.
We do not have much in
common,
this young Mary and I,
except that we shall both give
birth
to baby boys around the
same date.

She was poor,
a humble peasant girl.
I am rich,
especially by global standards.
She was an unwed mother,
outcast due to her pregnancy,
except by the honorable Joseph,
who was divinely persuaded
not to divorce her quietly.
I am happily married,
surrounded by the love
of a host of family and friends.
We do not have much in
common,
this young Mary and I.

She gave birth in a stable,
perhaps without much help.
I shall no doubt give birth
in a modern hospital,
surrounded by medical
personnel
and all the latest equipment.
She gave birth to the Christ,
the miraculous incarnation of
God's love.
I shall give birth to a very
human baby,
a miraculous mixture of his
parents'
strengths and weaknesses,
with a few of his own
thrown in.
We do not have much in
common,
this young Mary and I.
And yet perhaps there is one
thing:
the waiting.
She waited in anxiety and
anticipation
for her child to be born.
Thus I wait, and this Advent
season of
waiting takes on a double
meaning for me.

I have much to learn from Mary
about waiting.
She probably did it far better
than I.
I live in a world where I expect
fast foods, fast cars, and

situation comedies where the
whole plot
begins, unfolds, and is
completed
in thirty minutes
(with commercials). I am
impatient.
She lived in a world that seemed
to move
more slowly,
where days were filled
not with appointments and
meetings
but with the routine activities of
survival.
She probably knew how to wait.

And in that waiting,
she knew how
to say yes to God.
"I am a handmaid of the Lord;
let it be done
to me according to your word."
I, too, would say yes to God,
and yet too often I want that yes

to be on my terms and on my
schedule.
I need to learn from this young
Mary.

O God, in this season of
waiting,
as I prepare a cradle in the
nursery,
help me not to forget
to prepare a manger in my heart
so that Christ can once again be
born in me.

Help our church also to prepare,
as we give birth to our holiday
activities,
to again welcome Christ
as the center of our lives.

And help our world, O God,
as we struggle with
our many conflicting agendas,
to once again hear
the newborn cry of the Prince of
Peace.

Birth to Death

Lord, you have been our dwelling place in all
generations. Before the mountains were brought
forth, or ever you had formed the earth and the

world, from everlasting to everlasting you are God.
(Ps. 90:1–2)

In July 1989, I had the privilege of being with my maternal grandmother, Mamo, on her ninety-ninth birthday. It was my last such opportunity since her health was failing rapidly. She had the opportunity to meet our son, David. In those brief moments of being with her and of sharing our six-month-old baby with her, I was simply overwhelmed by the great mystery of the cycle of life.

As I thought of all the love she had shared with me—God's love—I recommitted myself to living out that kind of love, not just with our son but with all the children and adults whose paths crossed mine. To see how God had sustained her life and her love for almost a century, and to consider how I was now starting the whole cycle over in David's life, touched me deeply.

Christ Gives Peace

Peace I leave with you; my peace I give to you. I do not give to you as the world gives. Do not let your hearts be troubled, and do not let them be afraid.
(John 14:27)

It was the Saturday before Mother's Day in 1996. I had driven with a Knoxville church member to a church meeting in Cedar Rapids. For some reason, I didn't have my cell phone on, but when I arrived at the meeting the host pastor said, "You need to call Bob right away." My mother had been admitted to a hospital in Kansas the night before, so I was worried. Bob said, "Your mom has taken an unexpected turn for the worse. I've made you a reservation to fly out of Cedar Rapids this afternoon."

For the next few hours, I was stuck in that church meeting, and I was a mess. I have no memory of what the meeting was about. I was flooded with worry over my mom. The meeting leader periodically divided us into small groups to discuss some topic, but I couldn't do it. I couldn't muster the words to explain to the folks around me why I was such a mess. I just sat there looking distraught, crying on the inside.

As the host pastor kindly drove me to the airport, he tried to make pleasant conversation, but I was thinking, *How can we chitchat when my mother may be dying?* In fact, she did die that day—shortly before I arrived at her bedside. I didn't know that as I traveled, of course. I sat anxiously on the airplane, all alone, not knowing of my mother's condition and wondering how I could be helpful to her and to my dad.

At one point, I pulled out my calendar to see what the next week held. Sometimes a pastor's calendar can get pretty crowded with commitments that are challenging to change, but as I looked down at my calendar for the week ahead, I saw it was blank. And suddenly a peace came over me, as if Christ was saying, "I am giving you the time to do whatever you must do, and I am with you." Peace. My worry turned to prayer as I felt myself supported, carried by Christ's peace. Later, looking back on my experience and on my mom's death, I wrote this poem.

Good-bye, Mom

She could not wait to say good-bye,
Although I hurried so.
Through the skies, flying high,
The airplane went too slow.

Slowly Katie breathed her last.
She let go but not alone.
Surrounded by her two fine sons,
She made her journey home.

They said, "She would not have known you."

Their words are true, I'm sure.
But for many years, she did know us,
And that knowing will endure.

And so I say it now, dear Mom,
"Good-bye. I love you so.
Thank you for all you were to me.
We'll meet again, I know."

Thumbs up, she motions from afar.
"It's a date. I'll meet you here.
I am all right. I love you all.
Now wipe away the tears."

Grief Is Meant to Be Shared

> I will not leave you orphaned; I am coming to you.
> (John 14:18)

Shortly after Christmas in 1995, Bob and I replaced our basket of Christmas cards with what I came to call our sympathy basket. Soon that basket was overflowing with cards and well-wishes following the sudden death of Bob's twin brother, Bill, at the age of forty-nine. Shortly after Christmas, Bill died unexpectedly at home of ventricular fibrillation. We left the sympathy basket out where we could see it, as a reminder that many people were thinking of us in our grief.

In the spring of 1996, I bundled up the cards from Bill's death and told Bob, "I'm afraid I need this basket." The sympathy basket seemed to be a semi-permanent fixture in our home, as it filled anew with cards sent following my mother's death. The basket was a comfort to us. It reminded us that others cared. But it also was a reminder that losses sometimes come in succession and that we may wonder when the grief will ever end.

When I returned to Knoxville following my mother's death, I was still in shock. I dreaded attending church events; there were many due to a capital campaign for building renovations. *How can I endure it all?* I asked myself. But then I found an amazing thing happening to me.

Each time I was with my church family, I felt better. Members surrounded me with love and concern. We worshipped together, prayed together, and celebrated together. They were doing what they did so well—being a loving and caring community—and that made all the difference in the world to me. It wasn't long before someone said to me, "You're looking a lot better." And I knew I was.

For Better or for Worse

> Therefore a man leaves his father and his mother and clings to his wife, and they become one flesh. (Gen. 2:24)

Back in 1970, Bob and I said "I do" to the traditional wedding vows including phrases like "for better, for worse; for richer, for poorer; in sickness and in health." And over the years we've been reminded of the power of those unconditional proclamations of love.

For example, my natural hair color is light brown. However, in college, I heard blondes had more fun, so I became a blonde and remained one when Bob and I met. He thought he'd married a blonde! Shortly after we were married, I decided coloring my hair was a hassle and returned to my natural color. Bob was disappointed, and he complained, "What happened to my blond wife?" Because of Bob's bald head, I was able to respond, "Well, at least I *have* hair."

However, there was that season in 2004 when I didn't have *any* hair. I was undergoing chemotherapy for breast cancer, and all my hair fell out. I thought it was pretty crummy having no hair, but I had a supportive life companion who could speak from experience and say, "There are many things worse than not having hair." For better, for worse.

For richer, for poorer. Bob and I were married when he was still in law school. I didn't marry him because I thought he was going to be a rich lawyer. I married him because he was the finest person I had ever met, and he seemed to be crazy about me. But my father was very happy that I was marrying a lawyer. That said "financial security for my daughter" to my dad. I will never forget how concerned Dad was when Bob and I made the downwardly mobile decision to enter seminary. Bob had been practicing law for several years by that time. Dad called me when he knew Bob would not be around, asking, "Has Bob gone crazy?" Dad didn't have anything against the ministry, but he was worried about how we would support ourselves.

Bob and I often marvel at how we have always had enough money. With modest savings, no scholarships, and a part-time internship, we managed to complete four years of seminary with no debt. Although clergy salaries are modest, we always lived comfortably, finding that the more we gave away, the more we had to live on. Perhaps some time in the future we will experience the "for poorer" part of that classic wedding vow, but thus far we have always felt very rich.

Remembering What's Important

> I remember the days of old, I think about all your deeds, I meditate on the works of your hands. (Ps. 143:5)

All of us have the experience of forgetting things, whether it's names or important dates or appointments. Sometimes, as we age, the problem is not that we're distracted but that our brains simply can't function as they once did. We moved Bob's mom, Mayme Pearl

Ward, from Kansas to Iowa in 2008 when it became evident she was experiencing dementia. We were pleased to find an excellent assisted living facility nearby, specializing in memory care.

There are many kinds of memory loss and of dementia, and it has been interesting to walk alongside Bob's mother as she has dealt with hers. I've been most interested not in what she can't remember but in what she does remember, and what she remembers gives me quite a bit of hope.

Bob's mom has no short-term memory. She can't tell you what she had for lunch or what she did with her time that day. Although she enjoys reading, she has to choose short pieces like a daily devotional, because if she starts a book and puts it down, she won't remember what she read. She has never fully grasped that she is in Iowa and not in Kansas.

During her first few years in Iowa, her long-term memory was pretty good. She could remember family members and many life experiences up until a decade or so ago. Childhood experiences were the most vivid for her. While some of that has faded, she continues to remember Bob and sometimes recognizes me.

But more than events, I've noticed that Bob's mother remembers life lessons. She remembers the manners that were deeply ingrained in her. She remembers she was and is loved by other people and most important by God, and she is grateful. She's always giving thanks. She enjoys the beauty she sees around her, she delights in a good piece of chocolate, and she has a sense of humor. It seems to me these are some of the most important things!

Conclusion

For I am convinced that neither death, nor life, nor angels, nor rulers, nor things present, nor things to come, nor powers, nor height, nor depth, nor anything else in all creation, will be able to separate us from the love of God in Christ Jesus our Lord. (Rom. 8:38–39)

Life is a sequence of moments. In joyous times, spectacular moments seem to hurry by too quickly. In the routine of everyday life, ordinary moments often slip by unnoticed. During anxious moments, every minute seems to creep by at an agonizingly slow pace. But God is in each moment, and if we open ourselves to that reality, every moment is holy.

Reflections on my life experiences and on those of my loved ones remind me that in each moment, God offers us exactly what we need. Sometimes we miss that gift, perhaps because we're caught up in our own feelings, or we're in a hurry or we're preoccupied, or we foolishly turn a blind eye. But when we are open to God's loving presence, any moment can be full of grace. When we feel alone, God sends us the comfort of human community. When we fall short, we sometimes painfully understand that God is calling us to account. When we act with self-giving love, we feel a surge of joy from being in the flow of God's will. When we are in times of fear, we feel a loving power carrying us through.

So, as the apostle Paul said to the Romans, I must say I am convinced. Here's what I can enthusiastically say, based not just on what I have been taught or have read over the years but on the holy moments of my experience.

- Although we can never fully comprehend the full power and presence of God, God is real. There is a benevolent transcendent power in the universe.
- The nature of God is mercy and self-giving love.
- God is fully revealed in Jesus Christ, experienced today through the power of the Holy Spirit and made known most fully when the community of faith called the church faithfully follows Christ.
- God does not promise to fix our mistakes, heal our diseases, or solve our problems, but God does promise to be with us at every moment.

I don't have many assumptions about what happens to us after we die, but I believe our loving God will be with us then too. Thus, I close my reflections with the last words of John Wesley, who said from his deathbed at age eighty-eight, "Best of all is, God is with us."[1] Nothing can separate us from the love of God. I am convinced of that truth, and I hope that as you reflect on the holy moments of your life, you will be too.

—Martha D. Ward

Notes

Preface and Acknowledgments

1   Frederick Buechner, *The Alphabet of Grace* (Harper Collins, 1989), 3.

Chapter 1

1   Unless otherwise noted, all Scripture quotations are from *The New Revised Standard Version Bible*, copyright 1989, the Division of Christian Education of the National Council of the Churches of Christ in the United States of America. Used by permission. All rights reserved.

2   Mechtild of Magdeburg, "Praising God of Many Names," *The United Methodist Hymnal* (UM Publishing House, 1989), No. 104.

3   The King James Version of the Bible was originally published in 1611.

4   Robert Lowry, "My Life Flows On," *The Faith We Sing* (Abingdon Press, 2000), No. 2212.

Chapter 2

1   E. Stanley Jones, *Abundant Living* (Abingdon-Cokesbury Press, 1942), 63, 78, 117.

2   Larry Henley and Jeff Silbar, "Wind Beneath My Wings," 1982.

3   Mary Lou Redding, *Alive Now!*, May-June 1987, *The Upper Room*, 35.

Chapter 3

1   William Henry Ward, letter written to his sister, Estella, on July 19, 1862, from the camp of the 47th Ohio Volunteer Infantry at Meadow Bluff, Greenbrier County, Virginia.

Chapter 4

1   Abraham Lincoln, "Second Inaugural Address," delivered March 4, 1865, *Inaugural Addresses of the Presidents of the United States*, 1989, Bartelby.com.

2   Frederick W. Faber, "There's a Wideness in God's Mercy," *The United Methodist Hymnal* (UM Publishing House, 1989), No. 121.

Chapter 5

1   Curtis Mayfield, "People Get Ready," ABC-Paramount 10622, 1965.

Chapter 6

1   Meister Eckhart, www.beliefnet.com/wellness/2000/11/on-gratitude.aspx.

Chapter 7

1   Isaac Watts, "When I Survey the Wondrous Cross," *The United Methodist Hymnal* (UM Publishing House, 1989), No. 298.

Chapter 8

1   Pierre Teilhard de Chardin, *Toward the Future* (Harcourt Inc., 1936), 86–87.

Chapter 9

1   William Shakespeare, *Othello*, Act 3, Scene 3.

Chapter 10

1   Bruce Larson and Keith Miller, *The Edge of Adventure* (Word Press, 1974.)

Conclusion

1   J. F. Hurst, *John Wesley the Methodist* (Kessinger Publishing, 2003), 298.

Printed in the United States
By Bookmasters